JOB

STRATEGIES

for Professionals

A
Survival
Guide for
Experienced
White-Collar
Workers

Contributing Editor

J. Michael Farr

Project Director: Spring Dawn Reader
Editor: David F. Noble
Production Editor: Sara Adams
Cover Design: Robert Steven Pawlak
Interior Design: Peggy Emard
Composition/Layout: Spring Dawn Reader
Indexer: Joan Griffits

Job Strategies for Professionals—A Survival Guide for Experienced White-Collar Workers
©1994, JIST Works, Inc., Indianapolis, IN   **Reorder # JSSPRO**
Printed in the United States.

99 98 97 96 95 94   9 8 7 6 5 4 3 2 1

Send all inquiries to:
JIST Works, Inc.
720 North Park Avenue • Indianapolis, IN 46202-3431
Phone: (317) 264-3720 • FAX: (317) 264-3709

Library of Congress Cataloging-in-Publication Data
Farr, J. Michael,
    Job Strategies for Professionals : A Survival Guide for
Experienced White-Collar Workers / J. Michael Farr.
        p.   cm.
    "From JIST the Job Search People."
    Includes index.
    ISBN: 1-56370-139-1 : $9.95
    1. Job hunting—United States.   2. Professional employees—United
States.   3. White collar workers—United States.   I. Title.
HF5382.75.U6F369   1994
650.14—dc20   93-46886
                                                    CIP

1-56370-139-1

Foreword

This book is unique in many ways. It was written to fill the needs of the many experienced and trained individuals who have lost their jobs because of disruptions in the economy. It was developed by a group of specialists with experience in helping professionals, managers, college graduates, and experienced workers handle the loss of their jobs and their search for new ones. The need for such a book exists because many of the career planning and job search books available do not address the entire range of problems faced by unemployed professionals.

Because this book was developed by experts, it includes topics not covered in most job search books: for example, handling the grief and anger involved in job loss; financial planning; and the need for personal and family support. It also provides important job search information, including specific steps that job seekers can take to identify employment opportunities.

A job seeker can use the information in this guide to develop job hunting strategies, identify new job targets in different industries, and learn skills and techniques for successfully completing the applicant screening process.

We hope that you find this book useful. It presents a wealth of information in a clear, concise format. If you want more information on any of the topics covered, check the "Sources of Additional Information" listed at the end of the book for additional resource materials.

Acknowledgments

Much of this book was originally published by the United States Employment Service under the title *Job Search Guide: Strategies for Professionals*. Some sections of the text have been revised, but the basic structure of the original book remains intact. It is our belief that making this book available through commercial channels will increase access to this information. Following are the credits as they originally appeared in the U.S.E.S. edition:

The *Job Search Guide: Strategies for Professionals* was produced by the Assessment Research Development Program in the U.S. Employment Service under the direction of Robert A. Schaerfl, director. The Assessment Research Program is directed by Susan Schlickeisen, chief, Division of Planning and Operations. Coordination and technical supervision for the development of the *Job Search Guide* was directed by Russell Kile, personnel research psychologist. Grateful acknowledgment is also made for the contribution of additional technical planning and support by Kathleen Wiersema and David Rivkin of the Assessment Research Development Unit.

The Eastern Assessment Research Development Center, New York City, served a pivotal role in the planning, collection, preparation, and technical review of information for the guide, as well as its publication. The Arlington Employment Center, Arlington, Va staff reviewed the guide and gave valuable technical suggestions.

Space does not permit a listing of their names, but grateful acknowledgment is also given to those associations, business firms, labor organizations, other federal agencies, and individuals whose assistance and cooperation contributed significantly to the development of this publication.

Table of Contents

Introduction

L ooking for a job can be challenging and stimulating, but it can also be frustrating and stressful, even during the best economic conditions. In times of economic downturn, this task can become even more difficult as people compete for the chance to fill fewer jobs.

To gain the competitive edge when looking for a job, you will need to have your job search skills at their best. Whether you are involuntarily unemployed, changing jobs, or looking for your first job, this guide is designed to help you negotiate the many phases of the job search process.

Designed specifically for professionals, managers, college graduates, and executives, the guide presents an overview of important aspects of the job search, including handling your job loss, managing personal resources, self-assessment, researching the job market, networking, preparing your resume, and interviewing. A detailed list of sources that contain additional information is included so that you can do more research on any of the topics.

Chapters 1 and 2 provide guidance in dealing with personal, family, and financial issues that might arise during your job search.

In chapter 3 you can complete interactive exercises to assess your skills, interests, and abilities, and identify your achievements. This chapter directs you to resources that can help you match your particular talents and interests to the world of work.

Another important part of your job search is identifying industries and specific jobs that interest you. Chapter 4 identifies resources for targeting your job search and provides suggestions on how to research the job market and find the industries with the most opportunities. Chapter 5 presents both formal and informal methods for collecting information on specific companies that might have the right job for you.

Chapter 6 covers networking, one of the best methods for finding a job. Chapter 7 provides advice on writing resumes and cover letters, that can really make an impression on employers. (As most people know, almost all job screening includes some type of interview.) Chapter 8 presents different types of interviews, ways to prepare for an interview, and tips on how to conduct yourself during an interview.

Chapter 9 reviews assessment tools used by employers and is designed to help you feel more comfortable in testing situations. Brief descriptions of tests are provided, along with advice on how to prepare for and take the actual tests.

The last section of the guide helps you to review what you have learned. It provides questions to check your knowledge of the information presented in the guide. This will help you to ensure that you have planned and will conduct a well-thought-out, effective job search.

Tips for Using the Guide

Conducting a job search is a big job. This guide can provide excellent assistance in developing an effective job search strategy. Here are some general suggestions for using the guide that might make it easier for you to develop your job search plan.

Step 1. Review the entire guide.

Step 2. Find the chapters that really interest you. Remember, the guide can take you from the start to the finish of your job search. People who are not familiar with the job search process or who haven't conducted a job search for a long time, should follow the guide carefully from beginning to end. Those who are more comfortable with the job search might want to concentrate on those areas that are particularly relevant to their search.

Step 3. Identify specific tasks that you want to accomplish (e.g., identifying job leads, developing a resume, improving interviewing skills).

Step 4. Develop a timetable for completing tasks. Try to assign yourself weekly milestones. This way you will have intermediate goals to achieve on an almost daily basis.

Step 5. After completing an individual task, review what you have done. Determine how the task contributes to your overall strategy. Share your accomplishments with someone who might be able to give you constructive advice (a family member, friend, or counselor).

Step 6. Continue working through the guide until you feel comfortable with your job search strategy.

The guide has been designed to help you find satisfying employment. It provides a broad range of information that you can use to develop important job search skills and it serves as a reference to ensure that you are conducting an effective state-of-the-art job search.

Chapter 1
Handling Your Job Loss

While some people see a job loss as a challenge which opens up new opportunities, most associate losing a job with strong negative emotions. It is important to know that it is natural to have some negative feelings after a job loss, and that most people experience them. Here are some feelings and experiences that you may have after losing your job:

- **Loss of professional identity.** Professionals often identify strongly with their careers. Unemployment can lead to a loss of self-esteem. Being employed brings respect in the community and in the family. When a job is lost, part of your sense of self may be lost as well.

- **Loss of a network.** The loss may be worse when your social life has been strongly linked to your job. Many ongoing "work friendships" are suddenly severed. Old friends and colleagues often don't call because they feel awkward or don't know what to say. Some don't want to be reminded of what could happen to them. Also, when work and social activities mix, such as with company picnics and dinner parties, the job loss can be hard for all family members who participated in such activities.

1

■ **Emotional unpreparedness.** Those who have never been unemployed may not be emotionally prepared for a job loss and may be devastated when it happens. It is natural and appropriate to feel this way. Studies show that those who change jobs frequently and those in occupations prone to cyclic unemployment suffer far less emotional impact after job loss than those who have been steadily employed and who are unprepared for cutbacks.

This guide is designed to help you get over your loss and move forward in your quest for employment. As you work through the guide, completing tasks and accomplishing goals, your negative feelings should begin to be replaced with positive emotions.

Adjusting

One can begin adjusting to job loss by using a little psychology. Psychologists have found that people often have an easier time dealing with loss if they know what feelings to expect during the "grieving process." Grief usually doesn't overwhelm us all at once; often it is experienced in stages. The stages of loss or grief may include:

■ *Shock* is most likely the first stage. You may not be fully aware of what has happened.

■ *Denial* usually comes next. You cannot believe that the loss is true.

■ *Relief* then enters the picture for some. You feel a burden has lifted and opportunity awaits.

■ *Anger* often follows. You blame (often without cause) those you think are responsible, including yourself.

■ *Depression* may set in some time later, when you realize the reality of the loss.

■ *Acceptance* is the final stage of the process. You come to terms with the loss and get the energy and desire to move beyond it. The acceptance stage is the best place to be when starting a job search, but you may not have the luxury of waiting until this point to begin your search.

Knowing that a normal person will experience some predictable grieving reactions can help you deal with your loss in a constructive way. This book also will help you take steps to minimize the time it takes before you begin the constructive process of getting a new job.

College Graduates

People have always believed that finishing college would guarantee a good job and a solid future. Graduates looking for work in a tight labor market may experience just the opposite: You may have difficulty finding a professional job. The competition may be stiff, as more experienced, out-of-work professionals are vying for the same job. Rejection in the job search process can be very frustrating. Whether you were laid off from your last job or recently graduated from college, being unemployed and looking for work is emotionally difficult. You may experience periods of stress, depression, or erosion of self-esteem along the way.

Keep Healthy

Your body will be stressed as the challenges ahead test your strength and endurance. It is important to keep healthy and in shape. Try to:

- **Eat properly.** This helps you stay fit and healthy. How you look and your sense of self-esteem can be affected by your eating habits. It is easy to snack on junk food when you're home all day. Take time to plan your meals and snacks so they are well-balanced and nutritious. Eating properly will help you keep the good attitude you need during your job search.

- **Exercise.** Include some form of exercise as part of your daily activities. Regular exercise can reduce stress and depression and prevent a sense of lethargy. It can really help you get through those tough days.

- **Allow Time For Fun.** When you're planning your time, be sure to include time for fun and relaxation. You are allowed to enjoy life even if you are unemployed. Keep a list of activities or tasks that you want to accomplish, such as volunteer work, repairs around the house, or hobbies. When free time develops, you can refer to the list and have lots of things to do.

3

Family Issues

Unemployment is a stressful time for the entire family. Your family may experience adverse reactions to your job loss. For them, your unemployment means the loss of income and the fear of an uncertain future. They also are worried about your happiness. Here are some ways to get through this tough time together.

■ **Do not attempt to "shoulder" your problems alone.** Try to be open with family members. Discussions about your job search and your feelings allow your family to work as a group and support one another.

■ **Talk to your family.** Let them know your plans and activities. Share with them how you will be spending your time. Discuss what additional family responsibilities you can take on now while you're looking for a job and when your job search is complete. Add these new responsibilities to your schedule.

■ **Listen to your family.** Hear their concerns and their suggestions. Perhaps there are ways they can assist you.

■ **Build family spirit.** You will need a great deal of support from your family in the months ahead, but they will also need yours.

■ **Seek outside help.** Join a family support group. Many community centers, mental health agencies, and colleges have support groups for the unemployed and their families. These groups can provide a place to let off steam and share frustrations. They can also be a place to get ideas on how to survive this difficult period. More information about support groups is presented later in this chapter.

Helping Children

Children may be deeply affected by a parent's unemployment. It is important for them to know what has happened and how it will affect them. However, try not to overburden them with the responsibility of too many of the emotional or financial details.

■ **Keep an open dialogue with your children.** Letting them know what is really going on is vital. Children have a way of imagining the worst when they write their own "scripts," so the facts are often far less devastating than what they envision.

- **Make sure your children know it's not anybody's fault.** Children may think that *you* did something wrong to cause the job loss. Or they may feel that somehow *they* are responsible or financially burdensome. They need reassurance in these matters, regardless of their age.

- **Children need to feel they are helping.** They want to help, and having them do something like taking a cut in allowance, deferring expensive purchases, or getting an after-school job can make them feel as if they are part of the team.

- **Enlist help.** Some experts suggest that it is useful to alert the school counselor to your unemployment so that he or she can watch the children for problems at school.

Coping with Stress

Stress inevitably will be part of the job search process. Here are some coping mechanisms that can help you deal with stress.

- **Write down what seems to be causing the stress.** Identify the "stressors," then think of possible ways to handle each one. Can some demands be altered, lessened, or postponed? Can you live with any of them just as they are? Are there some that you could deal with more effectively?

- **Set priorities.** Deal with the most pressing needs or changes first. You cannot handle everything at once.

- **Establish a workable schedule.** When you set a schedule for yourself, make sure it is one which can be achieved. As you perform your tasks, you will feel a sense of control and accomplishment.

- **Reduce stress.** Learn relaxation and other stress-reduction techniques. This can be as simple as sitting in a chair, closing your eyes, taking a deep breath, and exhaling slowly while imagining all the tension going out with your breath. There are a number of other methods, including listening to relaxation tapes, which may help you cope with stress more effectively. Check the additional source material at the end of this guide for books which offer instruction on these techniques. (Many of these are available at your public library.)

- **Avoid isolation.** Keep in touch with your friends, even former co-workers, if you can do so comfortably. Unemployed individuals often feel a sense of isolation and loneliness. See your friends; talk with them; socialize with them. You are the same person you were before unemployment. The same goes for the activities that you enjoyed in the past. Evaluate them. Which can you afford to continue? If you find that your old hobbies or activities can't be part of your new budget scheme, perhaps you can substitute new activities that are less costly.

- **Join a support group.** No matter how understanding or caring your family or friends are, they may not be able to understand all that you're going through. You might be able to find help and understanding at a job-seeking support group.

  These groups consist of people who are going through the same experiences and emotions you are. Many groups also share tips on job opportunities, as well as feedback on ways to deal more effectively in the job search process. *The National Business Employment Weekly,* (available at major newsstands) lists support groups throughout the country. Local churches, YMCAs, YWCAs, and libraries often list (or even facilitate) support groups. A list of self-help groups (some of which cover the unemployed) is available from the National Self-Help Clearinghouse, 25 West 43rd St., Room 620, New York, NY, 10036. The cost is $1, plus a self-addressed, stamped envelope.

  Forty Plus, a national nonprofit organization, is an excellent source of information about clubs around the country and on issues concerning older employees and the job search process. The address is 15 Park Row, New York, NY, 10038. Their telephone number is (212) 233-6086.

Positive Mental Attitude Essential
You can expect to have negative emotions periodically during a long job search. But a positive mental attitude is essential in bringing the job search process to a satisfactory conclusion.

Keeping Your Spirits Up

Here are some ways to build your self-esteem and avoid depression:

- **List your positives.** Make a list of your positive qualities and your successes. It's easier to do this when you are feeling good about yourself. Perhaps you can enlist the assistance of a close friend or caring relative, or wait for a sunnier moment.

- **Replay your positives.** Once you have made this list, frequently replay the positives in your mind. Associate the replay with an activity you do often; for example, you might review the list every time you go to the refrigerator!

- **Use the list before performing difficult tasks.** Review the list when you are feeling down or to give you energy before you attempt some difficult task.

- **Recall successes.** Take time every day to recall a success.

- **Use realistic standards.** Avoid the trap of evaluating yourself using impossible standards that come from others. You are in a particular phase of your life; don't dwell on what you think society regards as success. Remind yourself that success will again be yours.

- **Know your strengths and weaknesses.** What things are you good at? What skills do you have? Do you need to learn new skills? Everyone has limitations. What are yours? Are there certain job duties that are just not right for you, and that you might want to avoid? Balance your limitations against your strong skills so that you don't let the negatives eat at your self-esteem. Incorporate this knowledge into your planning.

- **Picture success.** Practice visualizing positive results or outcomes. Play out a scene in your imagination and picture yourself successful in whatever you're about to attempt.

- **Build success.** Make a "to do" list. Include small, achievable tasks. Divide the tasks on your list and make a list for every day so that you will have some successes daily.

- **Surround yourself with positive people.** Socialize with family and friends who are supportive. You want to be around people who will "pick you up," not "knock you down." You know who your fans are. Try to find time to be around them.

■ **Volunteer.** Give something of yourself to others through volunteer work. It will help you to feel more worthwhile, and may actually give you new skills.

A New Beginning

As hard as it is to be out of work, it also can be a new beginning. A new direction may emerge which will change your life in positive ways. This may be a good time to reevaluate your attitudes and outlook.

■ **Live in the present.** The past is over and you cannot change it. Learn from your mistakes, and use that knowledge to plan for the future—then let the past go. Don't dwell on it. Don't be overpowered by guilt.

■ **Take responsibility for yourself.** Try not to complain or blame others. Save your energy for activities that result in positive experiences.

■ **Learn to accept what you cannot change.** However, realize that in most situations, you do have some control. Your reactions and your behavior are in your control and often will influence the outcome of events.

■ **Keep the job search under your own command.** This will give you a sense of control and prevent you from giving up and waiting for something to happen. Enlist everyone's aid in your job search, but make sure you do most of the work.

■ **Talk things out with people you trust.** Admit how you feel. For example, if you realize you're angry, find a positive way to vent it, perhaps through exercise.

■ **Face your fears, and try to pinpoint them.** Naming the "enemy" is the best strategy for relieving the vague feeling of anxiety. By facing what you actually fear, you can see how realistic your fears are.

■ **Think creatively, stay flexible, take risks, and don't be afraid of failure.** Try not to take rejection personally. Think of it as information that will help you later in your search. Take criticism as a way to learn more about yourself. Keep plugging away at the job search despite those inevitable setbacks. Most important, forget magic—what lies ahead is hard work!

Professional Help?

If your depression won't go away, or leads you to self-destructive behaviors such as abuse of alcohol or drugs, you may wish to consider asking a professional for help. Many people who have never sought professional assistance before find that in a time of crisis it really helps to talk to someone who can give needed aid. Consult your local mental health clinics, social services agencies, religious organization, or professional counselors for help for yourself and family members who are affected by your unemployment. Some assistance may be covered by your health insurance. If you do not have insurance, counseling often is available on a sliding scale fee based on income.

Chapter 2
Managing Your Personal Resources

Whether you are unemployed, working, or in school while you look for a job, your search will be more productive if it is well-planned. Start by making a list of the things you have to do. Deciding on career goals, updating your resume, doing library research, making phone calls, and arranging interviews are just some of the things you can do to start getting organized. Cross items off the list as they are completed to give yourself a sense of accomplishment.

Keep a Schedule

If you are employed or in school, set aside a specific portion of your day for job-hunting; don't just squeeze it in. On the other hand, don't risk losing a job or failing a course needed to graduate because of your job search.

- Set aside specific times for writing your resume, making phone calls, answering ads, and doing research.

- Use a calendar, daily planner (either electronic or paper), or your personal computer to keep track of your time and to make notes.

11

- Check your schedule every day. Don't rely on your memory.
- Set up a work space. Have a phone nearby. Keep a typewriter or computer, stationery, envelopes, stamps, copies of your resume, and phone directories handy. Choose a quiet space where you will be free from interruptions.

Sample Schedule

Here is a sample schedule for a typical day that one person created for job search and other activities.

WEDNESDAY, JULY 6
7:00 breakfast
8:00 read want ads
9:00 send out resumes
10:00 Call contacts for job leads
11:00 ↓
12:00 lunch
1:00 take pre-employment test at XYZ Company
2:00 ↓
3:00 meet job counselor at unemployment service
4:00 ↓
5:00
6:00 supper
7:00 research possible employers at library
8:00 ↓
9:00 send follow-up letters
10:00 read the Very Quick Job Search

Maintain a Routine

If you're unemployed, *job hunting is your new, full-time job.* Resist the temptation to sleep late or watch television all day. Plan to spend 30 to 40 hours per week on your job search. Your period of unemployment will be shorter if you make a concerted effort to find a new job.

- Get up in the morning and eat during the day at the same times as you did when you were working.
- Keep up with your exercise routine (or start one).

Stay on Top of Finances

Being unemployed probably means a substantially reduced personal income. Careful planning and money management will help you cope with changes in your financial situation. Some important things to do right away are:

- **Apply for benefits.** Apply for unemployment benefits as soon as possible, even if you're not sure you are eligible. If you do qualify, you can include the amount of your benefits in your monthly budget. Depending on how long you have worked, you can collect benefits for up to 26 weeks. In times of high unemployment, benefits may be available for a longer period. Contact your state labor department or employment security agency for further information.
- **Register with your local consumer credit counseling agency.** In some locations, you can register with a consumer credit counseling organization that will provide economic planning assistance and help you get a handle on your finances.
- **Examine your income and expenses.** Take a complete accounting of your income and expenses using the following chart as a guide:

Your Monthly Income/Expense Chart

INCOME		EXPENSES	
Unemployment benefits	____	Mortgage/rent	____
Spouse's income	____	Utilities: electric	____
Severance pay	____	Gas/fuel oil	____
Interest/dividends	____	Water	____
Other income	____	Telephone	____
		Food	____
TOTAL	____	Car payment/expenses	____
		Other loan payments	____
		Insurance premiums	____
		Medical expenses	____
		Tuition	____
		Clothing	____
		Entertainment	____
		Taxes	____
		Job hunting costs	____
		Other monthly expenses	____
		TOTAL	____

If you're like most people, your expenses exceed your income. You may have to dip into your assets, trim expenses, or both to make up the difference.

- **Review your assets.** Make a list of all your assets and their current value. The chart below can help:

ASSETS	VALUE
Liquid assets	
Checking/savings account	_____
Money market funds	_____
Pension/annuities/IRAs,	_____
Cash value of life insurance	_____
Securities	
Stocks/bonds/mutual funds	_____
Government securities	_____
Personal property	
Car(s)/boat	_____
Furniture/appliances	_____
Art/antiques/collectibles	_____
Jewelry/clothing	_____
Real estate	
Home	_____
Other properties	_____
Other assets	_____
TOTAL ASSETS	_____

Based on your monthly income-expense chart, see if it will be necessary to tap into your assets. Review your assets chart to see if you have enough to supplement your income for six months, nine months, or a year. When you have made this determination, you will know how much time you have to look for the job of your choice.

- Reassess your finances periodically. If your assets are being depleted and your ideal job has not yet come along, you may have to reevaluate your career goals, consider relocating, or take a "fill-in" job. Being a consultant might be an option for you. You might explore temporary jobs that typically are easier to obtain just to make money to help tide you over.

- **Reduce expenses.** In general, your strategy for controlling expenses will center on determining which costs are necessary to keep you and your family going and which are for conveniences or luxury items that you can reduce or do without. If you need to limit expenses, try some of the suggestions below:

  □ Reduce credit card purchases. Try to pay for things in cash to save on interest charges and to prevent overspending.

  □ Notify your bank or mortgage holder if you expect to have difficulty making mortgage or loan payments. They may be willing to renegotiate or arrange a better payment schedule.

  □ Consider cashing in some "luxury" assets. For example, sell a car or boat you rarely use. This not only generates cash but will save you money on insurance and maintenance costs.

  □ Comparison shop for home/auto/life and other insurance to make sure you have the best coverage at the lowest premium.

  □ Repair rather than replace major appliances.

  □ Keep your car well-maintained to avoid costly repairs.

  □ Cut down on utility expenses by washing full loads of clothes and dishes and by adjusting the thermostat and turning off lights and appliances that aren't being used.

  □ Reduce food costs by shopping for specials, using coupons, and cutting down on eating out.

  □ Enlist the cooperation of your spouse and children to help limit other family expenses.

- **Review your tax deductions.** Some job hunting expenses may be tax deductible as a "miscellaneous deduction" on your federal income tax return. According to the IRS,

  □ *"You may be able to deduct certain expenses you have in looking for a new job in your present occupation, even if you do not get a new job. You cannot deduct your expenses if you are looking for a job in a new occupation. ..."*

  If you are eligible, some of the expenses you may be able to deduct are employment agency fees, resume expenses, and some transportation expenses.

If you locate work in another city and you must relocate, some moving expenses are tax deductible on your federal tax return, Schedule A.

Keep records and receipts for all these expenses. Contact an accountant or the IRS for more information.

■ **Review your health coverage.** Although the cost of medical insurance is constantly increasing, it still is less expensive than becoming ill without insurance. There are several ways to obtain medical coverage for you and your family if you're out of work.

  □ You probably can maintain coverage, at your own expense, under the COBRA law if you worked for an employer that provided medical coverage and had 20 or more employees. Check with your former employer. To continue your health coverage under this law, you must tell your former employer within 60 days of leaving the job.

  □ If you are married and your spouse works, check to see if you can be covered under his or her health insurance plan.

  □ Contact any professional organizations you belong to; they may provide group coverage for their members. Speak to an insurance broker, if necessary, to arrange for health coverage on your own or join a local Health Maintenance Organization (HMO).

  □ Practice preventive medicine. The best way to save money on medical bills is to stay healthy. Try not to ignore minor ills. If they persist, phone or visit your doctor. It will be less costly to treat them before they become serious.

  □ Investigate local clinics. If you find that your health resources are being depleted, investigate local clinics that provide services based on a sliding scale. These clinics often provide quality health care at affordable prices.

Chapter 3
Assessing Your Skills, Experiences, and Interests

A successful job search starts with thorough preparation and planning. This is true whether you are beginning your career, seeking reemployment, or considering a more satisfying occupation. An important step in this process is to assess your personal characteristics; take a good look at who you are and what you have done. This will require time and effort, but the time you invest will be worthwhile. Self-assessment can help you to decide on a realistic job objective. The information will also be helpful when writing your resume, completing job applications, and preparing for job interviews.

Assessing Personal Information

The self-assessment worksheets on the next few pages will help you inventory your skills, knowledge, abilities, interests, accomplishments, values, and personal traits as they have been demonstrated in your day-to-day activities at work, school, home, and in the community. Make sure you include all your talents. Sometimes people take their biggest positives for granted. Have someone who knows you well review your worksheets to ensure you include all your positives. When completing the worksheets think about "transferables." These are skills and abilities that you can take with you to a new job. They are characteristics you have in which your new employer will be particularly interested. Remember, the employer is going to be looking for how you can benefit his or her organization.

> *A successful job search starts with thorough preparation and planning. This is true whether you are beginning your career, seeking re-employment or considering a more satisfying occupation.*

Use the following form to summarize your accomplishments, abilities, and personal characteristics. You should use a separate sheet, containing the same information, for each job you have held, including military service. If you have held different jobs with the same employer, you may want to handle each job separately. Make copies of the worksheet that follows, or create your own.

Work Experience

Organization: _____

Address: _____

Supervisor's name and title: _____

Dates of employment: _____

Position(s)/Title(s)/Military rank: _____

Duties and responsibilities: _____

_____

_____

_____

_____

_____

_____

Accomplishments (including awards or commendations): _____

_____

_____

_____

Skills, knowledge and abilities used (include "transferables"): _____

_____

_____

_____

_____

Duties liked and disliked: _____

_____

_____

_____

_____

_____

Reason for leaving: _____

_____

_____

Education and Training

School/College/University:_____

Dates of enrollment: _____

Major: _____

Degree or certificate:_____

Date:_____G.P.A.: _____

Career-related courses: _____

_____

_____

Scholastic honors, awards, and scholarships: _____

_____

_____

College extracurricular activities: _____

_____

_____

Other training (include courses sponsored by the military, employers, or professional associations): _____

_____

_____

Courses, activities liked and disliked: _____

_____

_____

Skills, knowledge and abilities learned: _____

_____

_____

Professional Licenses: _____

Personal Characteristics (e.g., organizational ability, study habits, social skills, like to work alone or on a team, like or dislike public speaking, detail work): _____

_____

_____

_____

Personal Activities

Professional (association memberships, positions held, committees served on, activities, honors, publications, patents): _____

_____

Community (civic, cultural, religious, political organization memberships; offices or positions held; activities): _____

_____

_____

Other (hobbies, recreational activities, and other personal abilities and accomplishments): _____

_____

_____

Overall Assessment

Take a look at each section of the worksheet you have completed: Work Experience, Education and Training, and Personal Activities. Considering all you have done, list your strengths and positive attributes in each of the areas below.

Skills, knowledge and abilities: _____

_____

_____

Accomplishments: _____

_____

_____

Personal characteristics: _____

_____

_____

Activities performed well: _____

_____

_____

Activities liked: _____

_____

_____

Career Possibilities to Explore

Review your assessment sheets. Do the strengths and positive attributes listed suggest possible careers for you? Your choice of a career need not be limited to the ones in which you have the most direct education, experience, or training. Ask yourself:

- Do I want to remain in that field?
- Would the strengths I have listed serve in a related field of work?
- Would I consider returning to school to learn new job skills which are in demand?
- As a recent college graduate, could I translate my strengths into a career?
- Is self-employment a possibility?

In answering these questions, carefully consider personal circumstances, your lifestyle, health, family circumstances, and financial needs. Keep these factors in mind when making career plans.

Considering everything you know about yourself, try to think of some career possibilities that you could do well and would enjoy. List these career possibilities below:

1. _____

2. _____

3. _____

4. _____

5. _____

You may obtain additional information about careers from a number of useful publications. Three examples, published by the Department of Labor or based on data they provide, are listed below:

- *Occupational Outlook Handbook* (OOH) presents useful information (including requirements, pay, and duties) for a wide variety of jobs. A bookstore version of this book, entitled *America's Top 300 Jobs*, provides the same information.
- *Guide for Occupational Exploration* (GOE) lists more than 12,000 occupations and organizes them into a structure developed specifically

for career guidance. It provides a wealth of information on how to relate your background to jobs and where to obtain additional information. Newer editions of this book—*The Complete Guide for Occupational Exploration* and *The Enhanced Guide for Occupational Exploration*—use the same structure and include details not found in the earlier GOE.

■ *Dictionary of Occupational Titles* (DOT) is the most comprehensive listing of job descriptions that exists. It describes more than 12,000 occupations and is used by many organizations (including all state employment service offices) to match people's qualifications to job openings.

These books are available at many libraries, college career centers, local employment service offices, and other locations. Some of the information may also be available to you through computer databases or bulletin boards. These and other sources of career information are described in more detail in chapter 4 of this guide.

If you are considering becoming self-employed or buying a franchise, the U.S. Small Business Administration (SBA) offers loans, training, and planning, as well as many useful publications. There are SBA offices in every state. Their toll-free number is 1-800-U ASK SBA. In addition, their Service Corps of Retired Executives (SCORE) provides free training and counseling on setting up and running a small business.

Two books on this topic are *Mind Your Own Business!—Getting Started as an Entrepreneur* by LaVerne Ludden and Bonnie Maitlen, and *The Directory of Franchise Opportunities*. Both are published by JIST Works, Inc.

Professional Assistance

If you want additional help in planning your career, there are many public and private career counseling services that can help you develop comprehensive career plans. You will find them listed in your local telephone directory. These organizations use a variety of tests and instruments to assess your skills, abilities, interests, and personality. Types of organizations where you can seek assistance include:

■ **State employment service offices.** These offices are located throughout the country. In most states, they provide career counseling services to those who are deciding on a career or thinking about changing careers. Many also provide interactive computer systems which contain job information. These services are free.

- **Local schools, community colleges, and libraries.** These organizations often have career counseling centers with computerized job and career information systems. Sometimes they offer short courses on conducting a job search. Some also offer counseling at no charge.

- **College/university guidance centers.** If you have graduated (or may soon graduate) from a college or university, consider the services offered by your college guidance center. College guidance centers sometimes offer their services to the public for a fee.

- **Nonprofit organizations.** Organizations such as the YMCA provide career counseling, although fees may be charged on a sliding scale. Check local social service agencies, community vocational services or religious organizations such as Catholic Social Services.

- **Privately run firms.** These firms provide counseling services useful in helping you decide on possible careers. However, they can be expensive and quality varies. Before you select one, check with the Better Business Bureau or with friends who have used the service.

Chapter 4
How to Research the Job Market

This chapter identifies some sources to help you research the job market for career fields that might be of interest to you. It can also help you identify companies that require your unique skills and abilities. By completing this chapter you will better be able to answer questions such as:

- How does the job market look for the career I have in mind?
- What are my chances of finding a position in that field?
- Should I consider relocating?

Where Will the Jobs Be?

The growth rate for jobs requiring higher-than-average levels of education and training is expected to outstrip the growth of jobs in general. However, it is also predicted that many companies will be downsizing, and many of the positions eliminated will be in middle management.

In general, growth in service-producing industries is expected to be much greater than growth in industries which produce goods. In manufacturing firms, however, employment in professional occupations is expected to grow slightly.

What size companies provide you with the best chance of being hired? Surprisingly, it has been estimated that two-thirds of all jobs are in smaller companies—those with 250 or fewer employees. Many of the publications mentioned later in this chapter concentrate on larger companies so it is also important to use the informal direct employer contact techniques discussed later to locate smaller businesses.

General Occupational Information

When deciding where to concentrate your job search efforts, it is useful to have data on industries which offer the best overall employment prospects.

If you have worked before, you are probably most familiar with one or two industries. Even if the outlooks for these industries are poor, you may well be able to find work if you make a concerted effort, as replacement workers are often needed. You probably will want to explore industries with better prospects as well.

If you are a first-time job seeker, there may be a number of different areas of work open to you, and it would certainly pay to concentrate on those with the highest potential.

Resources on the General Labor Market

Publications

There are a number of government and private publications which offer a wealth of information on outlooks, salaries, and growth trends for jobs and industries.

Most of these publications are for sale to individuals, and some of them are quite affordable. Many also are available as reference books in public libraries, in college and university libraries, counseling offices, and other locations.

Most large cities have branches of the public library which specialize in providing job information. These special libraries can be invaluable sources of labor market information. While in the library, don't rule out the librarian as a source of expert information.

Below are some examples of publications which are particularly good sources of labor market information. Those with an asterisk (∗) are available directly from the publisher, should you want your own copy.

- *Occupational Outlook Handbook (OOH)*. (Published every two years by the U.S. Department of Labor's Bureau of Labor Statistics.) Provides excellent descriptions of 250 of the most popular jobs, covering about 85% of the workforce. Well-written descriptions provide information on skills required, working conditions, duties, qualifications, pay, and advancement potential. The OOH helps in preparing for interviews by identifying key skills to emphasize.

- *America's Top 300 Jobs*. (JIST Works Inc., Indianapolis) This is a version of the *OOH* that is available from bookstores or in the circulation department of your library. Since the *OOH* itself is typically in the reference section of a library, this version allows you to access the same information at your leisure.

- *Career Guide to America's Top Industries*. (JIST Works Inc., Indianapolis) This book provides trends and other information on more than 40 major industries and summary data on many others. Written for the needs of people seeking jobs or making career plans, it is excellent for getting information on an industry prior to an interview. Includes details on employment projections, advancement opportunities, major trends, and a complete narrative description of each industry.

- *The Complete Guide for Occupational Exploration*. (JIST Works, Inc., Indianapolis) This book lists more than 12,000 job titles in a format that makes it easy to use for exploring career alternatives. Jobs with similar characteristics are grouped together with complete descriptions of skills required, nature of work, and other information. The *CGOE* also cross-references other standard reference sources for additional information on the jobs it lists.

- *The Enhanced Guide for Occupational Exploration*. (JIST Works, Inc., Indianapolis) A book using the same organizational structure as the *CGOE*, but including brief descriptions of about 2,500 jobs.

- *Dictionary of Occupational Titles*. (U.S. Department of Labor) Provides descriptions for more than 12,000 jobs, covering all jobs in our economy. This is the only book of its kind, and it can be used to identify jobs in different fields that use skills similar to those you have acquired in your past jobs. It also helps identify key skills to emphasize in interviews and provides brief descriptions for each job and additional coded information.

Specialized Publication Resources on the Labor Market

These publications provide more specialized information on the labor market. Larger libraries carry many of the resources, although some may be available only from more specialized libraries. For example, some libraries serve as a repository for government publications and others have special collections of career information. If your local library does not have the material, the librarian may be able to locate the materials at another library or arrange an interlibrary loan.

- *U.S. Industrial Outlook.* (U.S. Department of Commerce) Revised each year, provides business forecasts for more than 300 industries. Good source of information to review prior to interviews.

- *America's Federal Jobs.* (JIST Works, Inc., Indianapolis) Reviews more than 150 major departments in the federal government including information on each department's mission, divisions, available jobs, application procedures, and sources of additional information.

- *America's Top Military Careers.* (JIST Works, Inc., Indianapolis) Reviews about 200 military jobs, including type of work performed, employment, related jobs, and other details. Useful in finding skills that transfer from military jobs to civilian counterparts.

- *Other books in the "America's" Series. (JIST Works, Inc., Indianapolis) Each of the following provides thorough descriptions for about 60 of the top jobs in each area, career planning and job search tips, plus details on growth projections, education required, and other data on 500 additional jobs. Other titles in the series include:

    America's Top Technical and Trade Jobs
    America's 50 Fastest Growing Jobs
    America's Top Medical and Human Services Jobs
    America's Top Office, Management, and Sales Jobs
    America's Top Jobs for College Graduates

- *Projections 2000.* (U.S. Department of Labor) Provides detailed projections of the economy and labor force.

- *State and Metropolitan Area Data Book.* (U.S. Department of Commerce) Compiles statistical data from many public and private agencies. Includes unemployment rates, rate of employment growth and population growth for every state. Also presents data on employment and income for metropolitan areas across the country.

- *White Collar Pay: Private Goods-Producing Industries.* (U.S. Department of Labor's Bureau of Labor Statistics) Good source of salary information for white-collar jobs.

- *1991 AMS Office, Professional and Data Processing Salaries Report.* (Administrative Management Society, Washington DC) Salary distributions for 40 different occupations, many of which are professional. Subdivided by company size, type of business, region of the country, and by 41 different metropolitan areas.

- *American Salaries and Wages Survey.* (Gale Research, Detroit, Mich) Detailed information on salaries and wages for thousands of jobs. Data is subdivided geographically. Also gives cost-of-living data for selected areas, which is helpful in determining what the salary differences really mean. Provides information on numbers employed in each occupation, along with projected changes.

- *American Almanac of Jobs and Salaries.* (Avon Books, NY) Information on wages for specific occupations and job groups, many of which are professional and white-collar. Also presents trends in employment and wages.

Governmental Agencies

In addition to publications, there are several agencies that provide expert labor market information to the public without charge.

- **Bureau of Labor Statistics.** The U.S. Department of Labor's Bureau of Labor Statistics maintains eight regional offices around the country. Any of these offices may be contacted by phone during business hours to obtain labor market information for the area. The New York regional office also provides 24-hour access to recorded information covering such diverse topics as national and local employment statistics, wage information and how to get recent Bureau publications.

The telephone numbers of the Bureau of Labor Statistics regional offices are:

Boston	(617) 565-2327
New York	(212) 337-2400
Philadelphia	(215) 596-1154
Atlanta	(404) 347-4416
Chicago	(312) 353-1880
Dallas	(214) 767-6970
Kansas City	(816) 426-2481
San Francisco	(415) 744-6600

■ **State Occupational Information Coordinating Committee.** Each state maintains a State Occupational Information Coordinating Committee (SOICC), which helps the public locate labor market and career information and projections. The addresses and phone numbers for the SOICCs are listed in the *Occupational Outlook Handbook* or can be obtained from the National Occupational Information Coordinating Committee at (202) 653-5665.

Sources of Information on Specific Organizations

After you have a good idea of the industries, fields of work, and geographic areas where you want to concentrate your job search, the next step is to locate companies that employ people in your field.

Publications

There are many publications that contain lists of companies by industry, location, size, and other defining characteristics. Some of these are intended specifically to help job seekers; others are designed for different purposes. Regardless of the original intent, many of these publications can be used to find companies that may have potential for you. A few of them are discussed below.

■ *The Job Bank Series.* (Bob Adams Inc., Holbrook, Mass) A series of books aimed at job-seeking professionals, each covers a different large city or metropolitan area. Each book also gives an introductory economic outlook for the covered area, followed by a listing of the area's major companies. Common positions within the company are listed. General tips and advice on job hunting are provided.

- *The Job Hunter's Guide to 100 Great American Cities.* (Brattle Communications, Latham, NY) Rather than concentrating on a particular locale, this guide gives the principal-area employers for 100 of America's largest cities.

- *Macrae's State Industrial Directories.* (New York) Published for 15 northeastern states. Similar volumes are produced for other parts of the country by other publishers. Each book lists thousands of companies, concentrating on those that produce products rather than services. They include a large number of small firms, in addition to the larger ones listed in many other guides.

- *National Business Telephone Directory.* (Gale Research, Detroit, Mich) An alphabetical listing of companies across the United States, with their addresses and phone numbers. It includes many smaller firms (20 employees minimum).

- *Thomas Register.* (New York) Lists more than 100,000 companies across the country. Contains listings by company name, type of product made, and brand name of product produced. Catalogs provided by many of the companies also are included.

- *America's Fastest Growing Employers.* (Bob Adams Inc., Holbrook, Mass) Lists more than 700 of the fastest growing companies in the country. Also gives many tips on job hunting.

- *The Hidden Job Market: A Guide to America's 2000 Little-Known Fastest Growing High-Tech Companies.* (Peterson's Guides, Princeton, NJ) Concentrates on high-tech companies with good growth potential.

- *Dun & Bradstreet Million Dollar Directory.* (Parsippany, NJ) Provides information on 180,000 of the largest companies in the country. Gives the type of business, number of employees, and sales volume for each. It also lists the company's top executives. An abbreviated version of this publication also exists, which gives this information for the top 50,000 companies.

- *Standard & Poor's Register of Corporations, Directors and Executives.* (New York) Information similar to that in Dun and

Bradstreet's directory. Also contains a listing of the parent companies of subsidiaries and the interlocking affiliations of directors.

■ *The Career Guide—Dun's Employment Opportunities Directory.* (Parsippany, NJ) Aimed specifically at the professional job seeker. Lists more than 5,000 major U.S. companies which plan to recruit in the coming year. Unlike the other directories from Standard and Poor and Dun and Bradstreet, this guide lists personnel directors and gives information about firms' career opportunities and benefits packages. Also gives a state-by-state list of headhunters and tips on interviewing and resume writing.

There are many directories which give information about firms in a particular industry. A few samples are listed below:

■ *The Blue Book of Building and Construction*

■ *Directory of Advertising Agencies*

■ *Directory of Computer Dealers*

■ *McFadden American Bank Directory*

American Business Information, Inc. of Omaha, Nebr, publishes business directories for many different industries. They can be reached by phone at (402) 593-4600.

The local chambers of commerce and business associations may also publish directories listing companies within a specific geographic area. These are available in libraries or by writing to the individual associations.

And, of course, the *Yellow Pages* provides local listings of governmental and business organizations for every section of the country.

Professional and Trade Associations

These associations constitute another excellent avenue for getting information about where your kind of work might be found. These associations:

■ Help you identify areas where growth is occurring.

■ Provide the names of firms which employ people in a specific type of work.

- Identify the best information sources for developments within the field.
- Provide more information on small-firm leads than do directories.
- Publish newsletters with information on companies needing increased staff in the near future.

Some publications that list trade and professional associations are:

- *Encyclopedia of Associations.* (Gale Research, Detroit, Mich) A listing of more than 22,000 professional, trade, and nonprofit organizations in the United States.
- *Career Guide to Professional Associations.* (Garrett Park Press, Garrett Park, Md) Describes more than 2,500 professional associations. The information is more specifically oriented to the job seeker than is the *Encyclopedia of Associations.* A word of caution: because this guide has not been updated since 1980, some of the information may not be current.

Newspapers

Newspapers contain not only want ads but much other useful employment information. Articles about new or expanding companies can be valuable leads for new job possibilities.

If relocating is a possibility, look at newspapers from other areas. They can serve as a source of job leads as well as give some idea of the job market. Major out-of-town newspapers are sold in most large cities and also are available in many public libraries.

Some newspapers, such as *The New York Times, The Chicago Tribune*, and *The Financial Times*, are national in scope. *The National Business Employment Weekly*, published by *The Wall Street Journal*, contains much information of interest to professional job seekers.

Networking

Networking is another excellent way of gathering information about a particular field. It is one of the best ways of discovering smaller companies, which often are not listed in directories. Chapter 6 is devoted to tips and techniques on this subject.

Sources of International Labor Market Information

In an increasingly global economy, overseas employment is becoming a realistic alternative for many people. You may seek out overseas employment because you prefer exotic work locations, or you may consider foreign employment only after having difficulty finding work in the United States. In either case, looking for a job in the international labor market may open up many new employment possibilities.

- **Networking.** This is one of the best ways to get information about overseas work. Talk to anyone you know who has worked in the country in which you are interested. Another excellent method to find overseas opportunities is to look up companies which either are owned by a foreign parent firm or have foreign branches. There is a good chance you can find someone within the company who can advise you on the possibilities of foreign employment or at least refer you to the right authority. The company may even have an opening for you in a foreign location.

- **Newspapers.** Newspapers from foreign countries are available in most large cities. They carry want ads but, since citizenship and work requirements vary from country to country, many of the jobs listed may not be available to foreigners. A call or visit to the consul of the country in question may help you get some of this information. Many U.S. newspapers also carry ads for jobs overseas.

- **Directories and newsletters.** These sources list specific job openings in overseas firms. But be aware that by the time you reply to the opening it is likely to be filled.

- **International agencies.** These agencies maintain lists of consultants who are available to work overseas. Some agencies you might want to register with are:

  □ World Bank

  □ U.S. Aid for International Development (USAID)

  □ United Nations Development Program

  □ United Nations Industrial Development Organization (UNIDO)

- **The U.S. Government.** The federal government also has many jobs overseas. Don't overlook civil service announcements as a source of overseas employment. *Federal Career Opportunities* is available at most public libraries, and the publication *Federal News Digest* is available through subscription. State employment agencies offer computerized searches for federal job openings.

- **The Peace Corps.** This is another source of overseas jobs. Wages are low, living conditions may be less than optimal, but if you are interested in helping people, the Peace Corps may be a possibility.

- **Books and periodicals.** These sources provide useful information to the international job seeker.

  □ *How to Get a Job in Europe—The Insider's Guide.* (Surrey Books, Chicago) Gives country-by-country listings of newspapers, business directories, regulations, organizations, and other useful information.

  □ *How to Get a Job in the Pacific Rim.* (Surrey Books) Information similar to above, but for countries bordering the Pacific Ocean.

  □ *International Careers.* (Bob Adams, Inc., Holbrook, Mass) Information on finding work overseas. Covers government, private corporations, and nonprofit groups.

  □ *Passport to Overseas Employment—100,000 Job Opportunities Abroad.* (Prentice-Hall, Old Tappan, NJ) Information on overseas careers, study programs, and volunteer programs.

  □ *International Employment Hotline.* (Oakton, Va) Names and addresses of governmental and nongovernmental organizations hiring for overseas work.

  □ *Principal International Businesses.* (Dun & Bradstreet, Parsippany, NJ) An international version of the *Dun & Bradstreet Million Dollar Directory.* Although not aimed at the job seeker, it provides information on more than 55,000 companies in 143 different countries.

  □ *Key British Enterprises.* (Dun & Bradstreet) Detailed information on the 50,000 British companies which together employ more than a third of the British workforce.

  □ *Encyclopedia of Associations—International Organizations.* (Gale Research, Detroit) A listing of more than 11,000 non-profit

37

organizations in 180 countries. Includes trade, business, and commercial associations, and associations of labor unions.

☐ *Directory of European Industrial and Trade Associations.* (CBD Research, Kent, England) Industrial and trade associations of Europe. Gives the principal trade and activities in which each engages.

☐ *Directory of European Professional and Learned Societies.* (CBD Research) Similar in format to *Industrial and Trade Associations* above, but deals strictly with learned and professional societies.

Researching the international job market can give you many ideas about the careers, locations, and companies which look promising for overseas employment. Before you commit to an overseas job, however, carefully consider personal and family issues which might impede a full adjustment to your host country. Many companies expect at least a two-year commitment to an overseas job. Lack of foresight regarding cross-cultural adjustment could make it a very difficult two years.

Chapter 5

Getting the Most from Traditional and Nontraditional Job Search Methods

When you have decided the type of job for which you are best qualified, where you want to work, and which companies or organizations employ workers in your field, it is time to develop an effective strategy to find that job. People who develop an organized job search will have an easier time finding employment. This chapter will help you identify both formal and informal sources for locating job openings. It can even help you create a job opening where none currently exists.

How Do People Find Jobs?

Today's job seekers must develop their own contacts to find jobs.

The chart below shows the effectiveness of various job search methods based on the results of a U.S. Department of Labor study.

Effectiveness of Various Job Search Methods

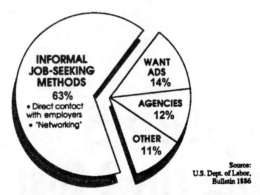

According to various studies, a vast majority of jobs (about two-thirds) are obtained using two "informal" methods: personal contacts (networking) and direct employer contacts. Only one-third of available openings are obtained using "formal" methods such as want ads, employment agencies, hiring halls, and civil service tests. Most job seekers probably spend too much of their time using formal methods, not realizing there are alternative methods.

You must carry out an active, as opposed to a passive, job search. It is not enough to respond to leads from want ads or employment agencies. Carrying out an active search allows you to control the job search process and opens up many more job opportunities.

Tapping the Hidden Job Market

Most job openings are part of the "hidden job market." The hidden job market consists of openings that are not yet advertised: jobs resulting from recent retirements, firings, company expansions, and anticipated future openings, along with jobs which do not currently exist but are created for individual job seekers. Most jobs never make it to the want ads or employment agencies; they are filled by people using direct contact methods. Employers usually use formal methods to advertise their jobs only when they are not filled through informal means.

In order to tap the hidden job market, a job seeker should spend most of his or her search time using informal methods. Most jobs are found through personal contacts or direct contacts with employers. The following sections describe how to begin using informal methods to tap the hidden job market.

Selecting Target Organizations

The first step is to compile a list of "target" companies or organizations where you might like to work. The organizations on the list may come from many sources. These include:

- Information obtained by researching the job market (including want ads and other sources);
- Personal knowledge about a company or organization or contacts you have within an organization;
- Lists of possible contacts through friends, relatives, and acquaintances;
- Information obtained through networking (covered in the next chapter);
- Listings of potential employers obtained from the *Yellow Pages*;
- Listings of potential employers obtained from directories and other sources.

Targeting Your List

If there are too many possible contacts on your list, start with a few of them. You might begin with organizations:

- About which you already know the most;
- About which you can readily get information;
- Where you have a contact;
- Where you would especially like to work.

As you learn more about these organizations, the list may change; some entries may be removed and others added. Once you have decided on a list of target organizations, you are ready to get to work.

Small Employers Are Important

As many as 70% of all workers in the private sector work in small businesses—those with 250 or fewer employees. While larger employers and the government remain important sources of jobs, most of the growth in jobs has been among small employers. Over the last decade, the largest of corporations have decreased the number of people they employ (often called "downsizing") while the number of workers has increased dramatically. Most of these new jobs have been created by small employers, and employers with fewer than 25 employees now create most of the new jobs.

For this reason, you should certainly consider looking for jobs with smaller employers. Some of the traditional job search techniques—such as applying at personnel offices and sending out unsolicited resumes—will not be effective with small employers. In many cases, small employers will not even have a personnel department, so you will often need to use nontraditional job search techniques to even find these employers.

Researching Your Target Organizations

Find out as much as you can about each of your target organizations. The information you will need includes answers to the following:

- What are the organization's products or services?
- What is the organization's status in its industry or field? Is the organization large or small, growing or downsizing?
- What can you learn about the job you want (the job duties, salary, benefits, work environment)?
- What is the public image of the organization, and what type of person "fits in?"
- What are some of the organization's current problems?
- Which people have the power to hire you?

Sources of Information about Your Target Organizations

- **Directories and publications.** Some examples are:
  - *The Job Bank Series*
  - *Thomas Register*

☐ *The Career Guide—Dun's Employment Opportunities Directory*

These, along with other publications, were described in more detail in chapter 4.

■ **Newspapers, business periodicals, trade and professional journals.** Review these sources for articles mentioning your target companies. Don't neglect specialty newspapers such as *The Wall Street Journal.* Look for information on new products, expansions, consolidations, relocations, promotions, articles by executives in the companies, annual company earnings, and current problems.

Check back issues of newspapers for old want ads. They can provide important information on job duties, salaries, and benefits. There may even be a want ad for a job in which you are interested. Perhaps the job was never filled or the person previously hired has already moved on.

■ **The organizations themselves.** If you are interested in a larger organization, call the human resources or public relations department. In smaller organizations, the receptionist or manager may be able to help. Get brochures, an annual report, description of relevant jobs, and anything else that describes the organization.

Making Contacts

■ If you want to be considered for a high-level job in an organization, go to the top managers, such as the CEO or senior vice president.

■ If you have an area of expertise, contact the manager of the department in your special area.

■ At smaller organizations, contact the owner, department head, or manager.

■ **Informational interview.** Meet with someone from the organization to get more detailed information about the organization itself and possibly a job lead. Informational interviews are discussed in chapter 6.

■ **Professional and trade associations.** Most professions and industries have their own trade associations. These associations may hold regular meetings and publish periodicals, both of which are good sources of inside information about members.

Many professionals belong to one or more professional associations. If you never joined yours, or your membership has expired, this might be a good time to get active. These organizations often have a membership directory, which is an excellent source of names for networking.

Professional groups usually have regular meetings, at which job openings may be posted. The association may also keep a resume bank or provide placement assistance to members. If your group does not have such services, suggest that they start one, and offer to help get it off the ground. That way you will be the first to hear of any interesting jobs.

Three methods commonly used to contact employees are **mail, phone**, and an **in-person visit.** Each of these are discussed in detail later in this chapter. The method that will work best for you with a particular organization depends on the information you uncovered during your research and how comfortable you are using the different contact methods.

Before using any of these methods, be sure to get the name (with the correct spelling and pronunciation) and the title of the person you are planning to contact.

If you were referred or obtained the information about whom to contact from someone you know, be sure to ask that person for permission to use their name. It always helps to say, "Mary Smith suggested I contact you...."

There Doesn't Have to Be a Job Opening!

One of the mistakes that many people make in their job search is to look for a job opening instead of looking for people who have the ability to hire or supervise someone with their skills—**even if there is no job opening now.**

While this seems to be a simple concept, it has profound implications. For example, it means that your search is for people who have the **potential** for hiring you, even if they don't have a job opening available right now. Instead of waiting for a job to be advertised, your task is to go out and find job openings that might not exist today—but will in the future.

Interviews for these situations may not be traditional interviews, but they will get you through many doors that most jobs seekers using traditional methods will never open. And when a job does open up—or is created for you—you are much less likely to be competing for it with many others.

Many jobs are, in fact, filled in this way. While you should certainly use traditional job seeking methods—and look for traditional interviews—you should also spend much of your job search time getting interviews with people who don't have a job opening now but **hire, need, or supervise people with skills similar to yours.** These contacts count as interviews too, and many people find that when a job does open up, these contacts may pay off. And, as you will learn in the next chapter, these contacts often can refer you to others who do know of or have openings now.

Mail Contacts

Mail campaigns are conducted by sending resumes or letters to your target companies or organizations. Various studies have found that sending out unsolicited resumes is not an effective way of getting interviews for most people. A better approach is to personally contact the prospective employer, ask for an interview, **then** send a resume.

Consider customizing your resume for each organization you contact and always compose an individualized cover letter. (See chapter 7 on writing resume and cover letters.)

Phone Contacts

Use the *Yellow Pages* to identify leads. Begin by reviewing the index in front, and review each entry. Ask this question for each one: "Might this type of organization use a person with my skills?" If the answer is "yes," mark that entry with either a 1 (if it sounds very interesting); 2 (if it sounds somewhat interesting); or 3 (if it does not sound interesting). If you do this for the entire index, you may end up with some unusual ideas for sources of leads as well as some that should be fairly obvious.

The next step is to turn to the section containing the index headings you selected as having potential. You may want to begin with the ones you marked as 2 or 3, so that you can practice your phone skills on these "less desirable" contacts. Of course, you might also uncover some interesting leads in this way, in places you would never have considered otherwise.

Prepare carefully before you make the call. Prepare a script; write down everything you want to say in words that reflect the way you speak. If you are calling an organization for the first time and do not have the name of a person to ask for, ask the receptionist for the name of the person in charge of the area most likely to need someone with your skills. In a smaller organization, simply ask to speak with the manager. Below is a suggested sequence to follow once you get past the receptionist to the person who has the hiring authority:

1. Introduce yourself. Tell the person what you do and how you can help the company or organization.

2. Discuss your accomplishments. For example, you can mention how you increased productivity that led to greater profits; created new and more efficient procedures that saved money; increased sales; or some other concrete statement.

3. State the reason for the phone call (to set up a meeting).

Here is a sample script:

"Good morning, Ms. Jones. My name is Martin Doe. I am an experienced marketing manager and would appreciate a few minutes of your time. I have read a great deal about your company, and I have some ideas that can help you get a larger share of the market. In my last job, I was able to use my abilities to obtain several new major accounts and increase sales by over 20 percent. When would be a good time to meet to discuss my ideas in more detail?"

Keep it brief. Your goal is to obtain an interview, even if there is no job opening. You are hoping that your knowledge of the firm and how you can assist them will convince the employer that he or she needs you.

Anticipate objections and prepare responses in advance. Some objections and possible responses are listed below:

Employer: I'm too busy to speak to you.

Response: I understand that you have a very busy schedule. When would be the best time to contact you?

If the employer won't give you a specific time, ask if you can send your resume so that he or she can look at it when they have a free moment.

Employer: You will have to speak to someone in the human resources department.

Response: That is fine. Whom should I ask for and is there a specific position that I should mention?

Employer: I don't need anyone with your skills right now.

Response: That's OK, I'd still like to see you to discuss the possibility of future openings.

Response: Perhaps I can send you a resume so you can keep me in mind for future openings. Do you know anyone else that may be able to use my abilities right now?

Practice the script so that it sounds spontaneous and unrehearsed. If you are nervous about calling, role play with a friend. You can also gain experience by making some of the first calls to companies or organizations that are low on your priority list. Don't feel that you have to stick to the script. Regardless of how much you prepare, you will probably have to adapt your responses to what is being said by the employer.

Talking to the Secretary

When you call an employer, you will probably speak first with a secretary. Be courteous and establish rapport with this important person. The secretary is your link to the employer and has information about the organization and job openings. If the employer isn't available, ask if there's a more convenient time to call back. Always be polite if the secretary will not put your call through. You might try calling again when the secretary might be out, perhaps after regular business hours or during lunch time.

In-Person Visit

Unannounced visits are not for the faint of heart but can be quite effective. Dress appropriately and be prepared for a job interview. Do all your research so that you know who you have to see. Getting to see someone may be somewhat easier in a smaller company, where the atmosphere usually is more informal and the person you want to see may be more accessible. If the person is busy, ask if you may wait. If this is not acceptable, leave a resume and call back in a few days to follow up.

As you travel to an interview, watch for other places along the way or even in the same building that might use a person with your skills. Simply drop in and ask to speak with the person in charge. Often this person will be willing to see you briefly or will schedule a time to see you later. Remember, you are not simply looking for a job that is open right now but want to be considered for any future openings. You also are looking for the names of others they may know who might know of openings.

Using Formal Job Search Methods

Although the majority of people find jobs through informal methods, formal methods are still important and should also be a part of your job search.

- **Want Ads.** Note that only 15% of people find their jobs through the want ads. Since virtually everyone who is looking for a job will read the same ads, the competition for the relatively few jobs that appeal to you will often be intense. Still, you should review the want ads on a regular basis as one source of job leads—but **not** as your most important source.

    Be familiar with the newspapers in cities where you want to work. Many libraries carry newspapers from other cities, and some newsstands specialize in this. Sunday and Wednesday papers typically have the most want ads. Be sure to check all sections which may have want ads. Publications that have want ads from all over the country include:

    - *The National Business Employment Weekly.* This has a compilation of the previous week's want ads from the regional editions of *The Wall Street Journal,* plus its own want ads.
    - *National Ad Search* is a weekly tabloid that has a compilation of want ads from 75 key newspapers across the U.S.
    - Want ads also may appear in professional and trade publications.

- **Using a Computer to Access Lists of Openings.** *Adnet Online* is a computer network which allows you to use a modem to browse through want ads for professional positions. It carries ads placed by companies throughout the United States and also has some international listings. The ads are updated twice a week, so the listings are quite current. *Adnet* has 1,500 to 2,000 positions offered at any one time. You can access it by subscribing to any of the following electronic information services:

- America Online (800) 827-6364
- Bix (800) 695-4775
- CompuServe (800) 848-8990
- GEnie (800) 638-9636
- PC-Link (800) 827-8532
- Promenade (800) 827-5938
- Prodigy (800) 776-0840

GEnie also has a function called *Dr. Job. Dr. Job* answers individual questions about career and employment issues through *GEnie's* electronic mail. Selected questions and answers also are published in a *Dr. Job* bulletin board.

- **Private Employment Agencies.** Private employment agencies are for-profit businesses that typically charge a fee. They may have job openings from a variety of companies. Some specialize in an area such as accounting, whereas others handle a large variety of jobs at various levels.

  Private agencies charge a fee either to you or to the employer who hires you. In some cases, this can be as high as 15% or more of your annual earnings. For this reason, it is obviously better to accept jobs for which the fee is paid by the employer. This fee typically is paid only if you get your job through the agency. Carefully review any agreements that you are asked to sign and get recommendations to find reliable agencies. Do not consider any agreement that requires you to pay a fee for jobs that you find on your own.

- **Temporary Agencies.** Some agencies specialize in placing you in temporary jobs. Since the employer pays the agency directly, there is typically no fee required from you. In some cases, these temporary jobs can lead to full-time job offers. Temporary jobs also can help you gain experience in a variety of different settings that may help you in later interviews and, of course, they can provide a temporary source of income while you conduct your job search.

■ **Employment Counseling Organizations and Firms.** There are a variety of self-employed individuals, community service organizations, and firms that provide career counseling and related services. Tax-supported organizations such as a community college may provide services for free or on a scale based on your income, whereas private firms and individuals will charge fees. Services might include testing, career planning assistance, help with resume preparation, training in job seeking skills, and other services. In some cases, fees for these services are quite reasonable, but in some cases they may cost thousands of dollars.

In general, avoid any service for which you feel pressured to sign an agreement for expensive services. In some cases, such services are overpriced and may even be misrepresented. If the services do sound like they can benefit you but the price seems high, you should shop for similar services from a variety of sources before making a decision, just as you would for many other expensive products or services. And be cautious in paying substantial amounts of money before services are rendered. If you pay everything up front, the incentive to please you is removed and you may have great difficulty getting back any part of your fee, even if you do not use the services.

More and more corporations are providing these types of services, from reputable firms, as part of their separation package. Since these "outplacement services" can be quite helpful, you should consider asking your previous employer to pay for them as part of your separation benefits.

■ **Executive Search Firms (Head-Hunters).** Executive search firms are hired and paid by employers to recruit for higher-level jobs. They do not typically charge the job seeker a fee. There are two categories: retainer and contingency.

□ **Retainer firms** are hired by individual employers to recruit for a specific position within the company. They often are consulted to help develop the candidate profile used as the basis for the search. Retainer firms work with the highest level professional jobs and are paid a retainer fee for the search even if they are unsuccessful in filling the position. They usually work with fewer employers than do contingency firms.

☐ **Contingency firms** work for several employers to recruit for various mid-level professional jobs. They are paid a fee only if they successfully fill a position.

Executive search firms are useful only to job seekers who have the experience profile that their clients desire. They prefer people who are currently employed but may consider you if you lost your job through no fault of your own. Contact some search firms which specialize in your industry. You probably will receive a better reception from contingency firms. When you call, state your experience briefly. If they are interested, they may ask you to send a resume or come in for an interview. During an interview, conduct yourself as you would with a prospective employer.

■ **Public Employment Agencies.** All states have a Department of Labor or a Bureau of Employment Security with offices located in major cities and towns. This is the same office where you apply for unemployment insurance benefits. They list job openings from many employers, including professional jobs. Some offer workshops in resume writing, job search skills, and interviewing techniques. These offices also may provide career counseling or career resource materials. In addition, they offer a computerized job bank which lists openings from around the country. All services are free. While many jobs will not be listed here, these offices are a source of potential leads and services. Consider using their services on a regular basis during your job search.

■ **College Placement Offices.** Most colleges have placement offices that provide a variety of services, including setting up interviews with corporate recruiters and listing job openings. Some provide job search workshops, resource materials, and other services for students as well as alumni. Check this out as one source of assistance.

■ **Alumni Associations.** Old schoolmates can be good sources of job leads and often are willing to help you if you simply ask. You can develop your own leads from the membership list of the alumni association. This is an excellent source of leads for people who live near you as well as those in other cities that you may target for your job search. Simply call them up and ask for help in identifying potential employers.

■ **Job Fairs.** A number of employers in a particular field will sometimes hold a job fair. These are advertised in local papers or trade journals and can give you an opportunity to meet recruiters from a variety of firms in a time-efficient way. Even if there is no appropriate job opening, job fairs give you the opportunity to gather important information about the participating companies, to inquire about future job openings for which you qualify, and to get the name and number of a representative for later follow-up.

Additional Job Search Resource Materials
*Refer to the end of this book for a listing of resource materials on job seeking skills, career planning, resume preparation, interviewing, and related topics. One book to consider is **The Very Quick Job Search.** (JIST Works, Inc.) Written by Mike Farr, it provides additional information on career planning and job search techniques and a proven approach to reducing the time it takes to find a job.*

Record Keeping

Keep a record of all your contacts. This will become particularly important for following up as you develop more leads than you can accurately remember. Use whatever method you find most convenient. A suggested format is illustrated in chapter 6. Your record should include the name, address, and telephone number of the target organization; the name of the person contacted; whether you called, visited, or sent a resume; what your next step is; when you should take it; and any other relevant information.

Use Multiple Methods

A thorough job search will use several methods simultaneously to uncover as many job leads as possible. One thing is true for all the approaches discussed here: The more you know about the targeted organization and how your skills and abilities can be used in their operations, the better your chances for success.

Chapter 6
Expanding Your Network of Contacts

Networking is the process of contacting people who can either give you information about potential job openings or introduce you to others who have this information. The ultimate goal of networking is to meet the person who has the authority to hire you for the job you want.

Why Networking?

As stated in the previous chapter, most jobs are never advertised in the newspaper or listed with employment agencies. Research indicates that one of the most effective ways of finding out about jobs is by getting leads from people you know: that is, by networking.

Even if most of the people you meet through networking don't know of a job for you, talking to them about your job search can help you clarify your job goals and hone your interviewing skills.

The people in your network also can give you emotional support, offer feedback on your job search techniques, and provide information about targeted organizations and trends in your field.

Who Is in Your Network?

Anyone you know who might have information about a job opening, or who **knows** someone who might have a lead about a job opening, is in your network. Friends and relatives are particularly important as a source of job leads, with almost 30% of all jobs being found through leads they provide. This is twice as many as those who find their jobs through the help wanted ads.

Acquaintances are another group of people you can develop as a source of job leads. In some cases (such as the members of your alumni association mentioned in the previous chapter) you may not know these people at all but have a common connection. Often that is enough to base a request for help from them in leading you to others who might have openings for a person with your skills.

Tell all of them that you're interested in exploring new job opportunities. Give them a brief review of your background. Be specific about what you're after. For example, say, "I'm looking for a job as a compensation analyst with a medium-sized firm," or "I'm a chemical engineer and I'd like to work in Saudi Arabia for awhile," rather than "I work in human resources," or "Do you know of any jobs?"

Who Is in Your Network?
• Parents & parents' friends • Children, spouse, & their friends • Aunts, uncles, & cousins • In-laws & former in-laws • Friends & neighbors • Professional colleagues • Present & former co-workers • Ex-college roommates & alumni • Former professors • Clergy • Social acquaintances • People at your health club • Local elected officials • Your doctor, accountant, lawyer, dentist, banker, barber, hairdresser, dry cleaner, shoemaker, and many others.

Make a list of each of the groups of people you know, beginning with your friends and relatives. Use a separate sheet of paper for each group, and list their names on one side and their phone numbers on the other. Then contact each one in an organized way, beginning with your friends and relatives.

While contacting people and asking for their help in your job search may sound intimidating, most people will be happy to help you if they can. If they don't know of any jobs at the moment, ask them to keep you in mind. Most importantly, ask them if they know two or three other people you can contact. Then contact those people and repeat the process.

Whenever you meet someone new, exchange business cards. Even if you're unemployed, have some cards printed; it is not very costly. Be sure to include your telephone number and profession. For example:

Celia Smith
Systems Analyst
Over 6 years of experience. Good communication skills, reliable, and can meet deadlines. Available immediately.
(313) 555-2222 to leave message

Send Thank-You Notes

Thank-you notes make a difference, and you should routinely send them out to all who help you during your job search. This includes those who simply gave you the name of someone to call as well as someone who is willing to see you for an interview. Also send them after an interview, and, if you want the job, say so in the note. Send these notes the same day you make contact or within 24 hours if possible.

Other Ways to Increase Your Network

- **Professional Contacts.** Besides following up with existing professional contacts, become active in a professional or trade association. Even if you are not now an active member, joining one or more professional organizations will give you access to their membership lists as a source of contacts. Their meetings or other events are also good opportunities for you to network with people in your field.

- **Civic and Religious Organizations.** Don't overlook these groups as sources of leads. If you have not been active, consider joining or becoming active. As you meet new people in the organization, you can network and work on a worthwhile project at the same time. You also can contact members of the organization and ask for their assistance in your job search by providing leads or ideas. Religious and community leaders often are willing to refer you to others in their congregation or their own networks who can offer you help, advice, or names of others to contact.

- **Follow Up Networking Leads.** After your initial networking efforts and research, you probably will have a long list of new people to contact. The next step is to meet with them to introduce yourself and get more information or job leads. If you happen to encounter someone on your list, you might be able to set up a meeting for a later date. However, most meetings are arranged by phone or mail.

- **Networking by Phone.** Most people you call will be happy to help you, but they may not have much time, so it's important to make your point directly and succinctly.

As described in chapter 5, write out a script ahead of time, but try to memorize rather than read it. Calling someone you don't know can be extremely stressful. If you are uncomfortable doing this, practice with a friend and get feedback on your presentation. When you're prepared, these calls will be easier than you anticipate. You have nothing to lose by calling. If you don't make the call, you'll never find out if there was good information or a job lead at the other end. If you do call, you may be successful. At the very worst, you'll feel a bit uncomfortable. Each call you make will make the next call easier and will prepare you for the more daunting task of calling an employer to ask for a job interview.

Use the sample below as a guide for making a networking phone call:

"Hello, Mr. Wise. My name is Bill Wynn. Martha Pabon suggested I speak to you about a career change I'm considering.

I was a financial analyst with Mammoth Bank for seven years. Since their merger, I've been exploring other options in finance and accounting.

I'd like to meet with you next week for about 20 to 30 minutes to get any advice you have to offer. Would Tuesday morning be convenient?"

- **Networking by Mail.** If you have many people to contact or are seeking a job in a distant city or overseas, developing a networking letter may be a good idea. The letter should be on your personal letterhead and include your address and telephone number. Like your phone calls, your letter should be brief and to the point. It is not a good idea to enclose your resume at this time, as you are not applying for a specific job opening. As with your phone calls, your mailing should be targeted, based on your networking and research, to those people or companies who are most likely to have the jobs or the information you seek.

Here is a sample of a networking letter written by someone who has not looked for a job in a long time and is seeking information about the employment outlook in his field. He has been referred by someone he has met by networking. A similar letter could also be sent without using a referral:

1234 Oak Drive
Albany, NY 12345
January 15, 19__

Ms. Marva Talent
The Art Workshop
1515 Willow Street
Buffalo, NY 14299

Dear Ms. Talent:

Mark Painter of All Right Advertising suggested I contact you for advice about my career plans.

I have worked as a designer for eight years at the Darling Clothing Company, which is going out of business shortly. As I have not had to look for a job recently, I would appreciate any information you can give me about the employment outlook for designers in the Buffalo area.

Could we arrange a brief meeting in the near future? I will call you early next week to set up an appointment.

Sincerely,

Raymond Best
(716) 999-2222

The sample below is a networking letter written by someone who wants to change careers and who is trying to establish a network in a new occupation:

9876 Elm Street
Detroit, MI 55555
June 1, 19__

Mr. Barry Bucks
President
Professional Fund Raisers of America
1000 Main Street
Chicago, Illinois 33333

Dear Mr. Bucks:

I have recently become a member of PFA and wanted to introduce myself to you.

After 20 successful years as a stockbroker, I am considering a career change. I have done a great deal of fund raising for my alma mater, Topnotch University, as well as for various local charities.

I believe that my selling ability along with my interest in fund raising point toward a career as a professional fund raiser. Before I proceed any further, I would like to meet with you to get your opinion about the advisability of such a career move.

I will call you next Thursday to arrange an appointment with you.

Sincerely,

Maria Candu
(312) 899-1111

The most important part of your networking letter is follow-up. If you say you will call someone next Thursday, **be sure to call!**

How to Keep Track of Your Networking Efforts

Keep a record of all the contacts you make, what the result was, and any follow-up that is needed. This will help you organize your time and monitor your progress. Review the job contact record that follows and use it as a guide in creating your own.

You may also want to keep a 3-by-5-inch card file for each person or company contacted. You can arrange these under dates for future follow-up. A card file system arranged by follow-up date becomes increasingly important as your number of contacts grows. If you have a computer, you may be able to use it to organize information about contacts and to help you schedule follow-up activities. Several computer software packages are commercially available to help in this process and may be purchased from a well-stocked software outlet.

Job Contact Record

Name	Nancy Vega	Martha Pabon	Arthur Wise	Angela Jones
Company/ Affiliation	Ace Employment Agency	Lee Financial	Fin'l Planners Inc.	U of M Placement office
Phone Number	587-7555	877-7700	923-4444	610-423-2020
Source of referral	Dentist— she's his wife	Uncle Jack's accountant	Martha Pabon	U of M Alumni News
Date of Contact	9/15-phone 10 am	9/15-phone 10 am	9/15-phone 10 am	9/15 by mail
Result	Appt. 9/16	Suggested I call Arthur Wise 923-4444	Info. Inter. 9/23 10 am	
Follow-up		Call 9/23 to let her know results		Call 9/30 if no word

Informational Interviewing

An information interview differs from a job search interview in that you are simply seeking advice. Informational interviewing is most useful if you are looking for your first job or want to change occupations. It also can be helpful to find out which companies are hiring and to find hidden jobs in organizations where you'd like to work.

Information interviews are less stressful than job interviews and are a good way to practice for them. However, if your only reason for visiting the company is to pursue a job lead, don't disguise your purpose by saying you want "information." If you know the jobs you want and the companies that have these jobs, skip informational interviews and try to arrange a job interview.

When interviewing for information, try to speak to the person who would have the power to hire you if there were an opening, or to someone who is doing the kind of work that you think you'd like to perform. When you meet with the people you've contacted by phone or letter, **you** are going to interview **them.** The informational interview consists of talking with people to get information about their occupation, company, or industry. **It is not a job interview,** although it may lead to a job offer.

Chapter 7
Writing Effective Resumes and Cover Letters

There is some controversy regarding resumes, with some experts saying that they are essential while others say that they are not nearly as important as most people believe. In most cases, employers will expect a resume from you, and, for this reason alone, it is worth doing. The controversy on resumes comes more from how they are **used**. The traditional advice in the past was to send out lots of unsolicited resumes. But this is not effective for most people. If you are conducting a traditional job search and are sending out unsolicited resumes to many organizations, you probably will be disappointed. Though almost any job search approach works for some people, resumes simply are not an effective tool for getting interviews. Direct contacts and leads provided by people you know are far better ways for most people to get interviews.

Despite their limitations, many employers do expect a resume and, if used correctly, it can be an important tool in your job search arsenal.

For these reasons, you will need to make certain that your resume presents you well.

What Does a Resume Accomplish?

A resume tells the prospective employer what you have accomplished in the past and what you can do for them now and in the future. The resume's primary function is to sell your experience, talents, and skills to an employer—clearly, forcefully, and quickly. In a sense, you are selling yourself and the resume is your advertisement.

In some situations—such as when you are competing with a large number of others or are being considered for a job in a larger organization—your resume may serve as your advance contact to awaken an employer's interest. Resumes also may be passed from one person to another (in and even outside an organization) and, in these situations, a resume is often the first contact a potential employer has with a job seeker. To be useful in these situations, your resume must make a good impression immediately.

Those who screen applicants responding to want ads or in large corporations use a resume as a screening device. A job may be advertised and large numbers of respondents apply, unsolicited resumes are received in the mail, and many (in a large organization) are submitted to the personnel department. Corporate personnel then give each resume a quick glance (10–20 seconds); discard those that do not have the needed experience, appear disorganized, or are too wordy (or some other criteria); and file the rest. If a job opening currently exists, those who appear to have the best credentials may be called in for a preliminary interview.

In this context, on the average, only one or two out of a hundred resumes will result in an interview. But employers still ask for resumes, and a good resume provides a competitive edge in the majority of professional, administrative, and managerial occupations. The task for you is to avoid getting your resume into a "stack" of resumes in the first place.

When Is a Resume Used?

There are many ways that you can use a resume during your job search. Some of these methods are more effective than others. The major traditional as well as some non-traditional methods are reviewed in this section. You will probably use more than one of the methods presented here, and the information should help you decide which approaches work best.

- **Mass Mailing Campaigns.** One traditional job search approach is to send a resume to each and every potential employer in an industry or selected geographic area. You may not know if the organization has a job opening, but you want them to know that you are available and that your experience and talents can be an asset to the firm.

  Mass mailings of this kind can be very expensive, and the odds of the approach resulting in interviews are slim. While the approach does occasionally work for some people—particularly if your skills are much in demand—there are more effective techniques. In most cases, you will be far better off in calling a potential employer first and requesting an interview, **then** sending a resume. But if you do choose to send unsolicited resumes, you can improve your chances of getting interviews by composing specific resumes for different organizations or types of organizations. For example, you could sort your targeted organizations into groups with similar characteristics and write a resume highlighting your appropriate strengths for each group.

- **Responding to a Want Ad.** Since hundreds or even thousands of people will read the same wants ads that you do, your odds of getting an interview are slim. Despite this, you should routinely respond to want ads that appear appropriate for you as one of your sources of job leads. In doing so, remember that most want ads result in many responses, and you should not expect personal acknowledgment of your resume in most cases.

  If possible, it is best to call the employer directly about the advertised job. Request to speak directly to the person who will supervise the position and request an interview. While this may seem aggressive, many employers value those who are creative in getting directly to them, and the chance of your getting an interview is greatly increased if you handle yourself well.

  Whether or not you call first, the most effective resumes are tailored for a particular employer. If the job requirements listed in the ad are vague or unclear, call the employer for more information. Try to get a clear picture of the job duties, education, and experience requirements. It's a good idea to list your questions in advance. Find out at the outset to whom you are speaking. Also try to find out the name and title of the individual who will review your resume. This will allow you to address a letter to that person and, perhaps, avoid the screening process before being considered by the person with the hiring authority. If you do get through to the hiring authority, ask for an interview directly. Then, of course, send a thank-you note along with a copy of your resume as soon as possible and before the interview.

- **Giving Resumes to People in Your Network.** It has already been noted that most people get their jobs through leads provided by friends, relatives, and acquaintances. Since these are the people who will help you the most, make sure that you give each one several copies of your resume. Invite them to give your resume to prospective employers or others they know who might also know of an opening. Let them know that you have plenty of additional copies of your resume and that they should call you if they need more.

  As your network expands, more and more of your resumes will be in circulation. Someone in your network may give your resume to a prospective employer you may never have contacted yourself. In this way, many people get interviews from a friend of a friend. Even prospective employers may pass along a copy of your resume to someone else following an interview or after talking to you on the phone. That is one reason to send thank-you notes, along with extra copies of your resume, following your contacts with anyone in your network.

- **Dropping Resumes Off to Employers.** Making direct contact with employers is an effective way to get interviews. Leave one or more copies of your resume behind with an employer if they are unable to see you at the time that you drop in. Then follow up with a phone call the next day and ask for the person who was to receive your resume. Ask for an interview.

- **Interviewing.** A well-done resume provides you with a variety of things to discuss in the interview. It can provide an outline of topics for both you and the employer. When you compose your resume, keep in mind that it gives you the chance to choose those topics you wish to discuss during the interview. For this reason, it is important to include strong examples of the skills and accomplishments you have which support your doing the job you seek.

What to Include on Your Resume

Be prepared to spend some time and effort in writing an effective resume. You will need two types of information:

1. **Information About Yourself.** You need a clear picture of your job talents, work history, education, and career goals. Look over the self-assessment list you completed in chapter 3 for this information. You also should refer to several reference books to review the skills you used in previously held jobs. Two excellent sources include the *Occupational Outlook Handbook* (OOH) and the *Dictionary of Occupational Titles* (DOT). Both are published by the U.S. Employment Service and are available in the reference section of most libraries. They provide generalized job descriptions of all the jobs you held in the past or those you wish to pursue in the future. A bookstore version of the OOH, entitled *America's Top 300 Jobs*, can be ordered from most bookstores or obtained in the circulation section of many libraries.

2. **About the Job.** Gather as much specific information as possible about the position for which you are applying. Your resume should show that your skills, education, work experience, and past job achievements are related to the position requirements. The OOH and DOT may be helpful here as well. Make sure that your resume emphasizes the skills, experiences, and accomplishments you have that most directly support the job you seek. Reviewing the OOH and DOT skills listed for past jobs and including them to support the skills indicated in the job you seek—and emphasizing these on your resume and in an interview—can help you tremendously in your job search.

Where to Get Additional Help

There are many sources of information on how to write a good resume.

- **Books.** There are as many variations in resume styles and formats as there are books on the market. Most books describe these variations in great detail and provide several examples. Some are specific to particular industries or to specific groups of job seekers.

  The Resume Solution, by David Swanson, is a particularly good source of information on creating a superior resume. It presents a step-by-step process for writing each section and creating a good-looking resume that will get attention. Several other good resume books are listed in the Sources of Additional Information at the end of this book. Most can be purchased through a local bookstore or obtained from a library.

- **Computer programs.** If you have access to a computer, there are several software programs to help you create and format a resume in the style of your choice. Check software listings at bookstores and computer stores.

- **Workshops.** Many workshops run by public and nonprofit agencies will help you write a resume. So will private, fee-charging firms. The quality of these workshops and the advice they provide varies widely based on the skill and knowledge of the presenter. In many cases, you can learn the same resume-writing tips from a good book, although the interaction with other job seekers and any personal assistance you receive may make these programs worthwhile.

- **Resume services.** Some services will help you revise and print your resume in a superior format. If you do not have access to a computer and a letter-quality or laser printer, these services are a good investment. More extensive services—including writing, editing, or revising your resume; career counseling; printing your resume on special papers with matching envelopes; and related services—are also available in most areas.

  Some of these services can be very helpful, particularly if you do not have experience in the special kind of writing, editing, and design skills needed to create a good resume. As with resume workshops, the skill and experience of the resume consultant is crucial, and you should consider references and several alternatives before spending money on these services.

After completing this chapter, you might want to refer to one of the resume books or other sources listed for additional information.

Types of Resumes

All of the resume styles described in books and computer programs are based on variations and combinations of two basic formats: **reverse chronological** and **functional.** One key to writing an effective resume is choosing the right style for you—one that emphasizes your strengths and deemphasizes your weaknesses. Whichever resume style you choose, make sure to include examples of results that you produced which benefitted your previous employers. Employers want to see measurable achievements. They want to know they are hiring someone who can contribute to their organization's bottom line.

> *Making Yourself More Marketable—Transferring Skills*
> *With the large numbers of people looking for well-paying jobs, competition has increased. To help prepare for this challenge, it is important to emphasize transferable skills. When you are thinking about your past work history (especially your most recent positions), consider the skills and responsibilities you had that you could perform on other jobs in different industries. For example, if you are in a sales or marketing position in the insurance industry, think about how you could apply those skills to the health care industry. The same is true for your accounting, computer, management, communication, analytical, and other skills. To get a better idea of transferable skills, look in the* **Occupational Outlook Handbook** *and the* **Dictionary of Occupational Titles.** *Both publications contain job descriptions which include lists of skills. By emphasizing transferable skills, you will open up your potential job market.*

The Chronological Resume

This format lists the jobs you've had by dates of employment. Because employers typically are most interested in your recent experience, a reverse chronological listing of previous jobs is recommended and presented in the examples in this book. The usual arrangement is: dates of employment; job title; name and address of previous employer; a brief description of the duties performed; skills used; and major accomplishments that benefitted your previous employers.

Use a chronological resume if:

■ You have progressed up a clearly defined career ladder and are looking for career advancement in the same field.

■ You have recent experience in the field you are seeking.

■ You have a continuous work history in your field.

Do not use if:

■ You have had many different types of jobs.

■ You have changed jobs frequently or have gaps in your employment history.

■ You are trying to change careers or switch fields.

■ You are just starting out.

An example of a reverse chronological resume can be found later in this chapter.

Tips for Preparing a Chronological Resume

■ List your most recent jobs first. Give dates for each job.

■ Briefly describe the main duties you performed and your accomplishments in each job.

■ Emphasize duties performed and past accomplishments that are important for the job you are currently seeking.

■ Emphasize performance and accomplishments, using numbers when possible.

■ Handle promotions as separate jobs.

Sample Chronological Resume

Robin Redding
947 Cherry Street
Middleville, OH 01234
(513) 987-6543

SUMMARY: Sales/Marketing professional with 12 years' progressively responsible experience with multi-outlet retailers. Demonstrated ability to motivate sales force and increase sales. Skilled in developing advertising campaigns and sales promotions.

EXPERIENCE:

Since 1994	Assistant to the Marketing Director, Colonial Kitchens, Inc., Columbus, OH. Supervised staff of 10, covering operations in three states. • Introduced new marketing techniques and set up training program for key staff to implement new procedures. • Developed promotional campaign, including yearly contest for naming new product styles. • Developed successful advertising campaign using radio and print media. • Increased sales an average of 30% in all market territory.
1991-94	Sales Director, Pots and Pans, Inc., Memphis, TN. Supervised sales staff in 15 outlets statewide. • Increased sales by 22%, profits by 9%. • Developed training programs and yearly goals for outlet managers. • Promoted goodwill by representing firm at community events, Chamber of Commerce, and charitable associations.
1988–91	Sales Manager, Nickel and Dime's Department Store, Kile, OH. Managed Hardware and Kitchenware Departments, supervised 13 sales personnel. • Ensured suitable display of merchandise on selling floor. • Analyzed trends and ensured availability of best-selling items. • Controlled inventory for two departments. • Directed changeover from manual to computer billing and inventory control. • Increased sales by 30% and departmental profits by over 40%.
EDUCATION:	Bachelor of Arts, Marketing, Ohio State University, OH. Averaged B+ in courses related to major and set new income records as head of student activities committee.
OTHER:	Worked my way through school with several jobs in retail sales including managing a small department store weekends and summers. Promoted several times in previous jobs and have excellent references. Am willing to work hard and have a track record of getting results.

69

The Functional Resume

Rather than employment dates and job titles, this format (sometimes called a "skills" resume) emphasizes your skills and accomplishments as they relate to the job for which you are applying. A functional resume presents a profile of your experience based on professional strengths or skill groupings.

A purely functional resume would not include many specifics about the dates of previous employment or other specifics of previous employers. For this reason, some people have used them to cover gaps in employment history, frequent job changes, a lack of formal education or other credentials, and other problems. Some employers do not like them because functional resumes often are used to hide a job seeker's problems, but this can be remedied (if you choose to do so) by including details of your employment history and other credentials in a separate section.

The distinct advantage of a functional resume format is that it allows you to present your particular strengths and to support your ability to do a particular job from a variety of work and non-work experiences. You can use a functional resume to present the case for your ability to do a job despite any weaknesses that might be displayed more obviously in a chronological resume.

Use a functional resume if:

- You have worked for only one employer, but have performed a wide variety of jobs.

- You are applying for a job that is different from your present or most recent job. For example, you may have recent military experience that does not have a clear civilian counterpart but does involve the use of many advanced skills.

- Your experience, education, or other credentials are not ideal. For example, if you have limited work experience related to the job you seek.

- You have gaps in your work history that you would prefer not to display obviously.

- You are re-entering the job market after several years of free-lancing, consulting, homemaking, or unemployment.

Do not use if:

■ Your work history is stable and continuous, because employers sometimes assume that a functional resume hides a spotty, unstable work history—unless you include a separate section that presents your chronological work history.

Each resume format has its advantages and disadvantages. Select the one that you think will present you most effectively or combine elements of both formats to suit your needs.

Tips for preparing a functional resume

■ Study the duties for the job you are seeking. Identify key skills that are important to the job.

■ Review your background and experience list from chapter 3. Find talents and accomplishments that demonstrate your ability to perform the job skills.

■ List your talents and accomplishments under the job skills to which they are related.

Sample Functional Resume
with Chronological Listing of Jobs Held

Robin Redding
947 Cherry Street
Middleville, OH 01234
(513) 987-6543

SUMMARY:	Sales/Marketing Director in the Retail Trade Industry
EXPERIENCE:	
SALES:	• Increased sales by 22%, using innovative techniques.
	• Developed training programs and yearly goals for sales managers in 15 outlet operations
	• Promoted goodwill by representing firm at community events, Chamber of Commerce, and charitable associations.
	• Ensured suitable display of merchandise on selling floor.
	• Directed changeover from manual to computer billing and inventory control.
MARKETING:	
	• Increased sales an average of 30% in market territory.
	• Supervised a staff of 10, covering operations in three states.
	• Introduced new marketing techniques and set up training program for key staff to implement new procedures.
	• Developed promotional campaign, including yearly contest for naming new product styles.
	• Developed successful advertising campaign using radio and print media.
WORK HISTORY:	
1994–Present	Assistant to the Marketing Director, Colonial Kitchens, Inc., Columbus, OH.
1991–94	Sales Director, Pots and Pans, Inc., Memphis, TN.
1988–91	Sales Manager, Nickel and Dime's Department Store, Kile, OH.
EDUCATION:	Bachelor of Arts, Marketing, Ohio State University. Averaged B+ in courses related to major and set new income records as head of student activities committee.
OTHER:	Worked my way through school with several jobs in retail sales including managing a small department store weekends and summers. Promoted several times in previous jobs and have excellent references. Am willing to work hard and have a track record of getting results.

72

Writing an Effective Resume

The following suggestions apply to any type of resume. The order below is recommended, but you can be flexible in creating your own resume.

Format

- **Heading.** Your name, address, and phone number should be prominently displayed at the top of the page. If you do not have an answering machine, consider including an additional phone number that will always be answered during the day. There is no need to head your page with "Resume" or another similar heading: The format will make it obvious.

- **Summary or Objective.** If you use a summary, highlight your experience and accomplishments in two or three sentences. Clearly communicate the type of job you want and what you can offer to an employer. If you prefer to state an objective, make it broad enough to embrace closely related jobs, but not so broad that you appear lacking in focus or willing to take anything. An objective should be only one sentence.

    Whether you choose a summary or an objective, indicate level, function, and industry for the position you are seeking. Be concise but general. Use your cover letter to make your summary or objective specific to a particular employer.

- **Experience.** Indicate your major responsibilities. Emphasize accomplishments and measurable benefits to your former employer: situations improved, savings/earnings, and new concepts adopted by firm. Achievements should be consistent with career direction, with a concentration on recent successes. When possible, use numbers to support your accomplishments, such as percentage of increased sales, employees supervised, and other objective measures.

- **Skills.** List special skills, such as word processing or an ability to operate special equipment.

- **Education.** Start with the most advanced degree and give name and location of the institution; major and minor fields; and all career-oriented scholarships and academic awards. Include career related extra-curricular activities, workshops, and seminars.

- **Licenses, Certifications, Publications.** Include only those that are career-related, without elaboration.
- **Additional Personal Data.** Include only if career-related, such as memberships in associations.
- **Make Every Word Count.** Most resumes should be one or two pages and no more. Make every word count and eliminate any content that does not directly support your ability to do the job.
- **Eliminate Errors.** An error in spelling or grammar on your resume will hurt you. Edit your resume several times to eliminate errors; then edit it again. Then give it to someone else to review. It is that important.
- **Make It Look Good.** Appearance counts. Take the time to create a good-looking resume with a simple, uncluttered appearance. Use only a letter-quality printer and print it on good quality paper.
- **Make Plenty of Copies.** While it is helpful to modify your resume for important interviews, it is not always possible. You will need to have resumes available to give to contacts in your network and for other uses. Have at least 50 to 100 done initially, and more as needed. Good quality photocopies are acceptable if done on quality paper, but a print shop can also print copies for a reasonable price. Ivory or off-white papers are recommended.

Content

DO:

- Be positive.
- Identify your relevant accomplishments. Use numbers to support your accomplishments where appropriate. Describe how they benefitted the employer.
- Have friends who know your professional accomplishments comment on your resume and suggest items you may have forgotten or dismissed as unimportant.
- Be specific. Choose words carefully; make every word count and eliminate unnecessary words.
- Use concise sentences. Use bullet entries for a clean, easy-to-read look.
- Use action verbs (see list, later in this chapter).

DON'T:

- Devote space to items not directly related to the job you are seeking, such as hobbies, personal data (height, weight, marital status), or descriptions of jobs that do not relate to your current objective.

- Explain employment gaps. If you have them, either don't include dates at all or include only general dates, such as "1991 to 1993," which avoid displaying, say, a three-month gap.

- Include references, or even a statement that they are available as an employer will ask for them if interested. However, a separate list of references should be prepared ahead of time, and these people should be informed that they may be contacted by prospective employers. You may also want to ask for letters of reference from previous employers as many organizations now refuse to provide information on past employees for fear of lawsuits.

- Include salary requirements, as these are often used to screen applicants.

Appearance

DO:

- Type or word-process your resume or have it professionally printed. If you use a computer printer, make sure the print is "letter quality." Use 8 1/2-by-11-inch quality white, ivory, or cream paper. If you can, use 20 pound weight, 100% cotton bond paper.

- Use wide margins. Single space within sections; double space between sections.

- Center or left-justify, and capitalize all headings.

- Make sure your resume "looks good"—neat, readable, symmetrical, and visually balanced. Stay away from needless, attention-getting visual effects.

- Proofread your resume carefully; then have someone else proofread it. Be sure your spelling, grammar, and punctuation are flawless.

- Inspect your resume for clarity. Smudges and marks are unacceptable.

DON'T:

- Use abbreviations, except for names of states.

Action Verbs

Action verbs give your resume power and direction. Skill statements that use action verbs help demonstrate to the potential employer responsibilities and initiatives you undertook on prior jobs. Following are samples of action verbs, organized within categories, that others have used in describing the tasks they performed.

Action Verbs

Management		
conducted	evaluated	presided
coordinated	facilitated	scheduled
developed	formulated	supervised
directed	guided	trained
established	improved	

Communication		
addressed	formulated	promoted
clarified	motivated	translated
conferred	negotiated	wrote
drafted	persuaded	
explained	presented	

Technical		
analyzed	examined	remodeled
assembled	identified	repaired
built	interpreted	researched
consulted	operated	revised
designed	overhauled	

Helping		
advised	counseled	instructed
arranged	diagnosed	oriented
coached	facilitated	represented

Creative		
conceptualized	fashioned	invented
created	illustrated	originated
designed	initiated	performed

Research

assessed	identified	summarized
designed	inspected	
evaluated	researched	

Financial

administered	calculated	planned
analyzed	contracted	projected
balanced	forecasted	recommended
budgeted	marketed	

Clerical

revised	compiled	prepared
collected	clarified	processed
catalogued	indexed	simplified
classified	organized	systemized

Sales

consolidated	increased	promoted
distributed	marketed	recruited
expedited	obtained	stimulated
generated	penetrated	

Cover Letter

Each time you mail your resume, include a cover letter stating your interest in the organization. The letter should not duplicate resume information. It should briefly highlight the skills or positions you held previously that are applicable to the position you seek. The letter also can add information that you think is important to the employer. Your cover letter should:

- Describe how your skills and abilities will benefit the organization.
- Peak the employer's interest.
- Request a job interview.

Below is a sample cover letter:

947 Cherry Street
Middleville, Ohio 01234
October 1, 1993

Mr. Alfred Newman, President
Alnew Consolidated Stores, Inc.
1 Newman Place
New City, OK 03033

Dear Mr. Newman:

I am interested in the position of national sales director which you recently advertised in the *Retail Sales and Marketing* newsletter.

I am very familiar with your company's innovative marketing techniques, as well as your enlightened policy in promoting and selling environmentally sound merchandise nationwide. I have been active for some time in environmental protection projects, both as a representative of my current employer and on my own. I recently successfully introduced a new line of kitchen products that exceeds federal standards, is environmentally safe, and is selling well.

The enclosed resume outlines my experience and skills in both sales and marketing in the retail field. I would like to meet with you to discuss how my skills would benefit Alnew Consolidated Stores. I will contact you soon to request an interview for current or future positions, and I can be reached at (513) 987-6543.

Thank you for your time and consideration.

Sincerely,

Robin Redding

Elements of a Cover Letter

- **Opening.** Explain why you are writing. State the position you are seeking and the source of the job opening (e.g., newspaper ad, professional organization, colleague).

- **Main body.** Highlight your job qualifications and link them to the organization's needs. Show that you know something about them and are interested in their products or services. Explain why you chose this organization. For example, you know someone who works there, you use their products, or you heard about their good reputation.

- **Closing.** Request an interview. Suggest a specific date and time. For example, "I'll try to contact you on Monday morning to see when you might be able to meet with me."

  □ Be sure to **include** your name, address, and telephone number.

  □ **Thank** the employer for his or her time and effort.

Tips on Preparing a Cover Letter

- Write an individualized cover letter for each employer.
- Address the letter to the person in the position to hire or supervise someone with your skills—the one most likely to make a hiring decision.
- Type or computer print letters on quality 8 1/2-by-11-inch paper.
- Use correct grammar, spelling, and punctuation.
- Convey personal warmth and enthusiasm.
- Keep your letter short and to the point.

Follow-Up

Keep a "tickler" file of the resumes you send out, and follow up with a phone call. Surveys have shown that only 2% of resumes mailed to employers result in an interview. If you follow up with a phone call, the success rate jumps to 20%.

Chapter 8
Interviewing Skills and Salary Negotiations

There are several types of interviews you may encounter. You probably won't know in advance which type you will be facing. Below are descriptions of the different types of interviews and what you can expect in each of them.

- **Screening Interview.** A preliminary interview either in person or by phone, in which a company representative determines whether you have the basic qualifications to warrant a subsequent interview.

- **Structured Interview.** The interviewer explores certain predetermined areas using questions written in advance. The interviewer has a written description of the experience, skills, and personality traits of an "ideal" candidate. Your experience and skills are compared to specific job tasks. This type of interview is common, and most traditional interviews are based on this format.

- **Unstructured Interview.** Although the interviewer is given a written description of the "ideal" candidate, he or she is not given instructions on what specific areas to cover.
- **Multiple Interviews.** These are commonly used with professional jobs. This approach involves a series of interviews in which you meet individually with various representatives of the organization. In the initial interview, the representative attempts to get basic information on your skills and abilities. In subsequent interviews, the focus is on how you would perform the job in relation to the company's goals and objectives.

    After the interviews are completed, the interviewers meet and pool their information about your qualifications for the job. A variation on this approach involves a series of interviews in which unsuitable candidates are screened out at each succeeding level.

Interviews Are Important
When there are many qualified candidates competing for the same position, how you do in the interview often determines whether you get the job.

- **Stress Interview.** The interviewer attempts to upset you, to see how you react under pressure. You may be asked questions that make you uncomfortable, or you may be interrupted when you are speaking. Although it is uncommon for an entire interview to be conducted under stress conditions, it is common for the interviewer to incorporate stress questions as a part of a traditional interview. (Examples of common stress questions are given later in this chapter).
- **Targeted Interview.** Although similar to the structured interview, the areas covered are more limited. Key qualifications for success on the job are identified, and relevant questions are prepared in advance.
- **Situational Interview.** Situations are set up which simulate common problems you may encounter on the job. Your responses to these situations are measured against predetermined standards. This approach often is used as one part of a traditional interview rather than as an entire interview format.

- **Group Interview.** You may be interviewed by two or more interviewers simultaneously. Sometimes one of the interviewers is designated to ask "stress" questions to see how you respond under pressure. A variation on this format is for two or more interviewers to interview a group of candidates at the same time.

The interview strategies discussed below can be used effectively in any type of interview you encounter.

Before the Interview

- **Prepare in Advance.** The better prepared you are, the less anxious you will be and the greater your chances will be for success.
- **Role Play.** Find someone to role play the interview with you. This person should be someone with whom you feel comfortable and with whom you can discuss your weaknesses freely. The person should be objective and knowledgeable, perhaps a business or professional associate.
- Use a mirror or video camera when you role play to see what kind of image you project.

Assess Your Interviewing Skills

- What are your strengths and weaknesses? Work on correcting your weaknesses, such as speaking rapidly, too loudly, or too softly, and nervous habits, such as trembling hands or inappropriate facial expressions.
- Learn the questions that are commonly asked and prepare answers to them. Examples of commonly asked interview questions are provided later in this chapter. Career centers and libraries often have books which include interview questions. Practice giving answers that are brief but thorough.
- Decide what questions you would like to ask and practice politely asking them at different points in the interview.

Evaluate Your Strengths

■ Evaluate your skills, abilities, and education as they relate to the type of job you are seeking.

■ If you have details about the specific job before the interview, practice tailoring your answers to show how you meet the organization's needs.

Assess Your Overall Appearance

■ Find out what clothing is appropriate for your industry. Although some industries (such as fashion and advertising) are more stylish, acceptable attire for most industries is conservative.

■ Have several sets of appropriate clothing available as you may have several interviews over a few days.

■ Your clothes should be clean and pressed, and your shoes should be polished.

■ Make sure your hair is neat, and your nails clean, and that you are generally well-groomed.

Research the Organization

The more you know about the organization and the job for which you are applying, the better you will do in the interview. Get as much information as you can before the interview (see chapter 4).

Have Extra Copies of Your Resume Available to Take to the Interview

The interviewer may ask you for extra copies. Make sure you bring along the same version of your resume that you originally sent. You also can refer to your resume to complete applications asking for job history information (e.g., dates of employment, names and telephone numbers of former employers, job responsibilities, and accomplishments).

Arrive Early for the Interview

Plan to arrive 10 to 15 minutes early. Give yourself time to find a restroom so you can check your appearance.

It's important to make a good impression from the moment you enter the reception area. Greet the receptionist cordially and try to appear confident. You never know what influence the receptionist has with your interviewer. With a little small talk, you may get some helpful information about the interviewer and the job opening. If you are asked to fill out an application while you're waiting, be sure to fill it out completely.

During the Interview

The job interview usually is a two-way discussion between you and a prospective employer. The interviewer is attempting to determine whether you have what they need, and you are attempting to determine if you will accept the job if is is offered. Both of you will be trying to get as much information as possible in order to make those decisions.

The interview that you are most likely to face is a structured interview with a traditional format. It usually consists of three phases: The **introductory phase** covers the greeting, small talk, and an overview of which areas will be discussed during the interview. The **middle phase** is a question-and-answer period. The interviewer asks most of the questions, but you are given an opportunity to ask questions as well. The **closing phase** gives you an opportunity to ask any final questions you may have, cover any important points that haven't been discussed, and get information about the next step in the process.

- **Introductory Phase.** This is very important. You want to make a good first impression and, if possible, get additional information you need about the job and the company.

  □ **Make a good impression.** You have only a few seconds to create a positive first impression, which can influence the rest of the interview and even determine whether you get the job.

    The interviewer's first impression of you is based mainly on nonverbal clues. The interviewer is assessing your overall appearance and demeanor. When greeting the interviewer, be sure your handshake is firm and that you make eye contact. Wait for the interviewer to signal you before you sit down.
    Once seated, your body language is very important in conveying a positive impression. Find a comfortable position so that you don't appear tense. Lean forward slightly and maintain eye contact with the interviewer. This posture shows that you are interested in what is being said. Smile naturally at appropriate times. Show that you are open and receptive by keeping your arms and legs uncrossed. Avoid keeping your briefcase or your handbag on your lap. Pace

your movements so that they are not too fast or too slow. Try to appear relaxed and confident.

- **Get the information you need.** If you weren't able to get complete information about the job and the organization in advance, try to get it as early as possible in the interview. Prepare your questions in advance. Knowing the following things will allow you to present those strengths and abilities that the employer wants:

  □ Why does the organization need someone in this position?

  □ Exactly what would they expect of you?

  □ Are they looking for traditional or innovative solutions to problems?

- **Know when to ask questions.** The problem with a traditional interview is that your chance to ask questions occurs late in the interview. How can you get the information you need early in the process without making the interviewer feel that you are taking control?

  Deciding exactly when to ask your questions is the tricky part. Timing is everything. You may have to make a decision based on intuition and your first impressions of the interviewer. Does the interviewer seem comfortable or nervous, soft-spoken or forceful, formal or casual? These signals will help you to judge the best time to ask your questions.

  The sooner you ask the questions, the less likely you are to disrupt the interviewer's agenda. However, if you ask questions too early, the interviewer may feel you are trying to control the interview.

  Try asking questions right after the greeting and small talk. Since most interviewers like to set the tone of the interview and maintain initial control, always phrase your questions in a way that leaves control with the interviewer. Perhaps say, "Would you mind telling me a little more about the job, so that I can focus on the information that would be most important to your organization?" If there is no job opening but you are trying to develop one, or if you need more information about the organization, try saying, "Could you tell me a little more about where your organization is going, so I can focus on those areas of my background that are most relevant?"

  You may want to wait until the interviewer has given an overview of what will be discussed. This overview may answer some of your questions or provide some details that you can use to ask additional questions. Once the middle phase of the interview has begun, you may find it more difficult to ask questions.

■ **Middle Phase.** During this phase of the interview, you will be asked questions about your work experience, skills, education, activities, and interests. You are being assessed on how you will perform the job in relation to the organization's objectives.

All your responses should be short and to the point. Use specific examples to illustrate your point whenever possible. Although your responses should be prepared in advance, so that they are well-phrased and effective, be sure they do not sound rehearsed. Remember that your responses must always be adapted to the present interview. Incorporate any information you obtained earlier in the interview with the responses you had prepared in advance and then answer in a way that is appropriate to the question.

Below are frequently asked interview questions and some suggested responses:

"Tell me about yourself."

Briefly describe your experience and background. If you are unsure what information the interviewer is seeking, say,

"Are there any areas in particular you'd like to know about?"

"What is your weakest point?" (A stress question)

Mention something that is actually a strength. Some examples:

"I'm something of a perfectionist."

"I'm a stickler for punctuality."

"I'm tenacious."

Give a specific situation from your previous job to illustrate your point.

"What is your strongest point?"

"I work well under pressure."

"I am organized and manage my time well."

If you do not have substantial experience in this field, you might say,

"I am eager to learn, and I don't have to unlearn old techniques."

Give a specific example to illustrate your point.

"What do you hope to be doing five years from now?"

"I hope I will still be working here and have increased my level of responsibility based on my performance and abilities."

"Why have you been out of work for so long?" (A stress question)

"I spent some time reevaluating my past experience and the current job market to see what direction I wanted to take."

"I had some offers, but I'm not just looking for another job; I'm looking for a career."

"What do you know about our organization? Why do you want to work here?"

This is where your research will come in handy.

"You are a small/large firm and a leading force in the local/national economy."

"Your organization is a leader in your field and growing."

"Your firm has a superior product/service."

You might try to get the interviewer to give you additional information about the organization by saying that you are very interested in learning more about their objectives. This will help you to focus your response on relevant areas.

"What is your greatest accomplishment?"

Give a specific illustration from your previous or current job, such as where you saved money or helped increase profits. If you have limited work experience in the field, find some accomplishment from previous jobs, your school work, part-time jobs, or extra-curricular activities.

"Why should we hire you?" (A stress question)

> Ultimately, this is the most important question for you to answer well. Highlight your background based on the organization's current needs. Recap your qualifications, keeping the interviewer's job description in mind. If you don't have much experience in this industry, talk about how your other experience, education, and training prepared you for this job.

"Why do you want to make a change now?"

> *"I want to develop my potential."*

> *"The opportunities in my present organization are limited."*

"Tell me about a problem you had in your last job, and how you resolved it."

> The employer may want to assess your analytical skills and see if you are a team player. Select a problem from your last job and explain how you solved it.

Some questions you should ask:

- ☐ What are the organization's current challenges?
- ☐ Could you give me a more detailed job description?
- ☐ Why is this position open?
- ☐ Are there opportunities for advancement?
- ☐ To whom would I report?

- ■ **Closing Phase.** During the closing phase of an interview, you will be asked whether you have any other questions. Ask any relevant question that has not yet been answered. Highlight any of your strengths that have not been discussed. If another interview is to be scheduled, get the necessary information. If this is the final interview, find out when the decision is to be made and when you can call. If you do want this job, now is the time to say so and to present your reasons for wanting **and** being able to do the job. Thank the interviewer by name and say goodbye.

Illegal Questions

There is a variety of laws that govern what an employer can consider in making a decision to hire one person over another. It is illegal for an

89

interviewer to discriminate based on gender, age, race, religion, national origin, or marital status, or to ask questions about your personal life that are not job-related. It is also now illegal to avoid hiring people with certain handicaps if they are able to do the job. What can you do if you are asked a question that you think is designed to screen you based on one of these issues? Before reacting, take a moment to evaluate the situation. Ask yourself these questions:

- How uncomfortable has this question made me feel?
- Does the interviewer seem unaware that the question is illegal?
- Is this interviewer going to be my boss?

Then respond in a way that is comfortable for you. If you decide to answer the question, provide a brief response and try to move the conversation back to an examination of your skills and abilities as quickly as possible. For example, if asked about your age, you might reply, "I'm in my forties, and I have a wealth of experience that would be an asset to your organization."

If you are not sure whether you want to answer the question, first ask for a clarification of how this question relates to your qualifications for the job. You may decide to answer if there is a reasonable explanation. If you feel there is no justification for the question, you might say that you do not see the relationship between the question and your qualifications for the job and you prefer not to answer it. Of course, doing this may jeopardize your being considered for this job. If you think that is the case, there are legal steps you can take to keep this employer from using inappropriate screening criteria.

During the Interview

DO:
- Be sincere and direct.
- Be attentive and polite.
- Ask relevant questions.
- Answer questions briefly.
- Use specific examples to illustrate points.

DON'T:
- Smoke or chew gum.
- Try to control the entire interview.

- Bring up salary, benefits, or working hours.
- Be too serious.
- Let your depression or discouragement show.
- Make negative comments about anyone or anything, including former employers.
- Look at your watch.
- Take extensive notes.

After the Interview

You are not finished yet. It is important to assess the interview shortly after it is concluded. Following your interview you should:

- Write down the name and title (be sure the spelling is correct) of the interviewer.
- Review what the job requires and record what the next step will be.
- Note your reactions to the interview; include what went well and what went poorly.
- Assess what you learned from the experience and how you can improve your performance in future interviews.

Make sure you send a **thank-you note** within 24 hours. Your **thank-you note** should:

- Be hand-written only if you have very good handwriting. Most people type the thank-you note.
- Be on good quality white or cream-colored paper.
- Be simple and brief.
- Express your appreciation for the interviewer's time.
- Show enthusiasm for the job.
- Get across that you want the job and can do it.

Few people send a thank-you note or letter after an interview. Make sure you are one of those few—it could give you the edge.

Here is a sample thank-you letter:

July 20, 1993

Dear Mr. Adams:

I really appreciated your taking the time to meet with me this afternoon. I believe that my experience in dealing with new products would fit right in with your marketing plan. I am very interested in working for your company.

As we agreed, you will hear from me next Thursday.

Sincerely,
Gail Strong

Follow Up with a Phone Call

This is not a time to be shy. If you want the job, you should say so in your thank-you letter and you should consider calling after the interview. Use your judgment in when to call. In some cases, you may want to call within 24 hours to ask a question or to say that you are definitely interested.

At that time, if you learn that the decision has not been made, find out whether you are still under consideration for the job. Ask if there are any other questions the interviewer might have about your qualifications, and offer to come in for another interview if necessary. If the job interests you, this is one more time to say so—and to tell why you can do the job.

If you learn that you did not get the job, try to find out why. You might also inquire whether the interviewer can think of anyone else who might be able to use someone with your abilities, either in another department or at another organization.

If you are offered the job, you have to decide whether you want it. (*See* Negotiating Your Compensation Package later in this chapter.) Never turn down a job offer when it is first given! Even if it does not pay your minimum salary or has other deficiencies, do not turn it down immediately. If you are not sure, thank the employer for the offer and ask for one to several days to think about it. Ask any other questions you might need answered to help you with the decision. In doing so, remember that most employers will want a quick and firm acceptance or they will go on to another applicant.

If you know you want the job and have all the information you need, this is your last chance to negotiate salary and other details. In doing so, be careful not to jeopardize a good offer by being too demanding or acting as if you do not want the job. Once you have settled on the terms, accept the job with thanks and get the details on when you start. Ask whether the employer will be sending a letter of confirmation, as it is best to have the offer in writing.

Who Gets Hired?

In the final analysis, employers will hire someone who has the abilities and talents which fulfill their needs. It is up to you to demonstrate at the interview that you are the person they want.

Negotiating Your Compensation Package

Do not discuss your specific compensation package, especially salary, with the employer until you have been offered the job and you think it is an offer you should seriously consider. During salary negotiations, you are not only discussing your pay but your entire compensation package. This includes vacation time, sick leave, health insurance, tuition reimbursement, and other benefits.

Your base salary and any performance-based raises are probably the most negotiable parts of your compensation package. However, some organizations have a cafeteria approach to benefits in which you select from a number of benefit options based on a total monetary cost. In other words, they will spend a certain amount of money on each employee for benefits, and employees have some flexibility on which benefit options they select. For example, employees with children might select a child care reimbursement benefit, whereas employees interested in going back to school might choose tuition reimbursement. When negotiating your compensation package, it is important to keep in mind the total package. Make sure you consider all benefits, not just salary. Before you begin negotiating your compensation, decide which benefits are most important to you so that you are ready to talk to the employer.

Salary Negotiations

Like other parts of the job search process, the key to salary negotiations is preparation. It is important for you to do your research before you begin. In order to determine the salary you are willing to

93

accept, investigate the salary range someone with your skills and experience can expect to receive.

How do you find salary information?

- **The library.** Your local library should have a number of references for finding the salary ranges for the occupation you are considering. Some reference books include:

  □ *State and Metropolitan Area Data Book.* (Published by the U.S. Department of Commerce) Compiles statistical data from many public and private agencies. Includes unemployment rates, rate of employment growth, and population growth for every state. Also presents a vast amount of data on employment and income for metropolitan areas across the country.

  □ *White Collar Pay: Private Goods-Producing Industries.* (Produced by the U.S. Department of Labor's Bureau of Labor Statistics) Good source of salary information for white-collar jobs.

  □ *1991 AMS Office, Professional and Data Processing Salaries Report.* (Administrative Management Society, Washington DC) Salary distributions for 40 different occupations, many of which are professional. Subdivided by company size, type of business, region of the country, and by 41 different metropolitan areas.

  □ *American Salaries and Wages Survey.* (Gale Research, Detroit) Detailed information on salaries and wages for thousands of jobs. Data is subdivided geographically. Also gives cost-of-living data for selected areas, which is helpful in determining what the salary differences mean. Provides information on numbers employed in each occupation, along with projected changes.

  □ *American Almanac of Jobs and Salaries.* (Avon Books, New York) Information on wages for specific occupations and job groups, many of which are professional and white-collar. Also presents trends in employment and wages.

  Ask the reference librarian for assistance in locating other salary information resources.

- **Professional associations.** National and regional professional associations frequently conduct salary surveys. They ask people in the "profession" what compensation they are receiving. Contact your

94

professional association and ask if they can provide you with salary information.

- **Your network.** Talk to colleagues in your professional network. Although people often don't want to tell you what they are making, usually they are willing to talk about salary ranges. Ask colleagues, based on their experience, what salary range you might expect for the position.

- **Job search centers.** These centers (which can be found in schools, libraries, community centers, or as part of federal, state, or local government programs) frequently keep salary information on hand.

- **Your past experience.** If you are applying for a job in a field in which you have experience, you probably have a good idea of what someone with your skills and abilities should be paid. Think about your past salary. Unless the job you are applying for requires dramatically different responsibilities than your former position, your previous salary is a good starting point for salary negotiation.

The Negotiation Meeting

Once you have an idea of the salary and benefits you are willing to accept, it's time to negotiate. Don't sell yourself short during these negotiations. Usually, when an organization is ready to make you an offer they have invested a lot of time and money in their search for a qualified employee. You don't want to be overly aggressive with the employer, but you do want to receive a fair compensation package.

If the employer makes you an offer that does not seem reasonable, discuss your concerns with him or her. Present these concerns in a constructive, nonthreatening manner. Focus on why you have concerns, as opposed to making general statements about "what you deserve." For example, it won't be productive to simply state, "I must have more money." It will be more productive to explain that the offer is less than you were making previously and you would like them to match your previous salary. In most situations, employers do have some flexibility in what they can offer an applicant. They might be able to offer you more money or compensate you with additional benefits (for example, more vacation leave). Some organizations can offer a signing bonus to compensate for other "weaknesses" in their package.

When you are considering the offer, make sure you are taking into account the entire benefits package. Sometimes excellent benefits can compensate for a lower salary. If you really want the job but the offer still seems low after negotiations, see if the employer will consider a salary review three to six months from your starting date. Also, usually you don't have to make a decision about the offer immediately. It is legitimate to ask for a day or so to give serious consideration to the offer, but do so only if you feel it is necessary, as some employers may see this as a sign of disinterest and offer the job to someone else.

If you do come to an agreement with the employer, find out when you can expect to receive the offer in writing. It is important to get the official offer documented. An official letter usually means that the "higher ups" have approved your offer.

Chapter 9
Employment Tests and Other Screening Systems

Some employers use tests or other assessment tools as part of their screening process. In most instances, these instruments are given as part of the screening process, but sometimes they are given after you are hired. Below is a listing and brief descriptions of the types of assessment tools that employers may use.

Ability Tests

Ability tests are designed to predict future success in both job training and job performance. Employers use these tests to evaluate your potential to learn and perform particular job responsibilities. Although ability tests seldom are used for job applicants who are professionally trained or hold advanced degrees, you may encounter them as part of the screening process. Some employers administer ability tests after hiring an applicant to determine specific placement within the organization.

Two types of ability tests that employers administer are:

■ **General Ability Tests** measure general abilities such as verbal, mathematical and reasoning skills. These are skills that contribute to success in many different types of jobs. For example, many professional jobs require you to read and comprehend written material, so the employer might administer an ability test to measure this skill.

■ **Specific Ability Tests** measure more narrowly defined abilities directly related to specific areas of job performance. For example, you might be asked to take a mechanical ability test if you are applying for an engineering position or a job with an architectural firm. Or you may be required to take a computer skills test to measure your knowledge of computer software or systems the job requires.

Usually, both types of ability tests are timed and in a multiple choice format. You probably took similar kinds of tests in high school or when you applied to college. You can't study for ability tests, but you might familiarize yourself with the testing process by taking tests from textbooks or test preparation books. Work within time limits to get comfortable with the testing process.

Skills Testing

Skills tests can measure specifically what you know about and can perform in a particular job. These tests are designed to test your mastery of tasks. Employers administer skills tests when they want to hire someone who can "hit the ground running" and perform the job as soon as he or she starts. These tests usually are given to people applying for nonmanagerial positions.

Skills tests can be in a **written** or **work sample** format. If the test is in a **written format,** you will be asked specific questions about particular job tasks. For example, if you are taking a skills test for tax accountants, you may be asked questions about filling out tax forms. Or if you are applying for a personnel position, you may be asked about conducting an interview.

If the test is in a **work sample format,** you will actually perform portions of the job. For example, if you are applying for the tax accountant position, you will actually complete a tax form. If you are applying for the personnel position, you will actually conduct the interview.

You can prepare for skills tests by "studying up" and practicing skills that you think are important to the job for which you are applying. For example, if you took courses in college that apply to the job, you might reread some of your notes or review textbooks. Or you might review projects that you completed in a former job that related directly to the new position.

Assessment Centers

If you are being considered for a professional or managerial position, the employer might send you through an assessment center. Here you will be asked to complete several standardized exercises designed to simulate job situations. These exercises measure higher level management, problem-solving, and decision-making skills. Examples of assessment center exercises include:

- **In-basket test.** You are asked to sit at a desk and sort through materials left in an in-basket. Based on the information presented, you might be asked to prioritize work responsibilities, make recommendations for a plan of action, or solve a specific problem. You also might be asked to provide a written response to the in-basket exercise or to present a verbal response.

- **Leaderless group discussion.** You and a group of applicants are asked to solve a problem. Your performance is evaluated based on the behaviors you exhibit during the discussion. The employer might be trying to evaluate your leadership abilities, looking at whether you take a lead role in the discussion. He or she will also watch to see if you are a good team player and seem to interact well with other group members.

- **Role-play exercise.** You are asked to meet with a "mock employee" and help that employee solve a particular problem. The employee usually is played by an assessment center facilitator. Before you meet with the employee, you are given background information on the problem. Examples of situations you might be asked to deal with are tardiness, missed deadlines, or problems related to a particular work project. Your performance is judged on behaviors demonstrated, advice given, or how well you helped the employee solve the problem.

Assessment centers are expensive to set up so they are used mostly by larger public and private sector companies. However, in recent years assessment centers have gained in popularity. Many private consulting firms have been set up to design assessment center exercises. So even if you are applying to a smaller company, you may be asked to participate in assessment center-type exercises.

Personality and Interest Inventories

Employers administer these types of measures when they are looking for applicants with particular interests or personality traits, and because they have found that employees with these characteristics are successful on the job.

Unlike ability tests, personality and interest inventories attempt to assess noncognitive, underlying characteristics. These inventories can help an employer evaluate your motives, needs, values, goals, or dispositions. Personality inventories such as the Myers-Briggs Type Indicator® (MBTI)[1], the California Psychological Inventory, and the Hogan Personality Inventory can be used to assess self-confidence, sociability, and flexibility. Interest inventories such as the Strong Interest Inventory, the Career Exploration Inventory, or Holland's Self-Directed Search are used to determine your interests in various career areas or whether you are creative, social, enterprising, or investigative.

Unlike other types of tests used for personnel selection, there are no right or wrong answers to personality and interest inventories. You are asked to answer questions about things you like or do not like. For example, you might be asked what type of activities you like to do in your spare time, or if you prefer working with groups of people, or by yourself.

Employers can use personality and interest inventories to assess your creativity, leadership abilities, or level of self-esteem. When completing a personality or interest inventory, you might notice that some of the questions seem similar or are simply being asked in a different way. Repeated or rephrased questions are included to ensure that you are answering questions truthfully.

---

1 *Myers-Briggs Type Indicator* and MBTI are registered trademarks of Consulting Psychologists Press, Inc.

Honesty or Integrity Tests

Employee theft is an increasing concern in many organizations. In today's competitive marketplace, employers do not want to worry about employees who are dishonest. Employers are particularly concerned about hiring "honest" employees when their job responsibilities include handling cash or merchandise.

To help ensure that the employees they hire are honest, employers may administer integrity tests. There are two types of questions asked on these tests. The first asks about illegal or dishonest behaviors you may have exhibited in the past. For example, you might be asked if you have ever walked out of a restaurant without paying the bill. The second type asks about your attitudes toward dishonest behavior. For example, you might be asked your views on punishing shoplifters. On an integrity test, you also might be asked questions about past involvement with drugs or alcohol.

Like personality and interest inventories, questions sometimes are repeated on integrity tests to check for "faking." Also, studies have shown that on many integrity tests, it is difficult to cheat; in other words, it is difficult for the applicant to figure out which is the "right" answer. Like all selection instruments, the best way to respond to questions is in a truthful, professional manner.

Some General Tips for Taking Tests

- Get a good night's sleep.
- If you're sick, call and reschedule the test.
- Get to the test site early.
- Tell the administrator if you have any physical difficulties that might impair your test performance.
- Make sure to bring your eyeglasses, hearing aid, and anything else you might need.
- Bring several number 2 pencils with good erasers and an erasable pen.
- If you don't understand the test instructions, ask for assistance before the test begins.
- Don't linger over difficult questions. Work as quickly as you can without making mistakes.

- Find out if guessing is penalized. If there is no penalty, guess when you don't know the answer to a question.
- Ask about the retesting policy. There is a possibility you can retake the test if you feel you did not do well.

Medical Examinations

Medical exams are given to determine if you have a physical condition which prevents you from performing the job. The Americans with Disabilities Act (ADA) gives people with some disabilities certain rights to prevent an employer from unjustly rejecting them for a job that they can do. This prevents such practices as asking about disabilities on an application form or using preemployment physicals as a screening mechanism, although physical exams can be given after a job has been offered.

If you have a disability or a medical condition which you think may pose barriers to your being hired, your state Vocational Rehabilitation Agency can offer assistance.

Drug Tests

Drug tests indicate the presence of illegal drugs. An increasing number of employers are using drug tests to screen candidates for all job categories, including managers and professionals. You should be aware that some medications, and even some foods, can produce a positive reading even if you have used no illegal drugs. It is important to inform the employer of any medications you have taken recently. Also be aware that drug tests may not be completely accurate. If you are told that your sample indicated drug use but you know you haven't used any illegal substances, ask if there is a formal appeals process. Tell them that you would like to take the test again. Perhaps you can ask if there is another, more sophisticated test you can take.

Appendix I

Staying Employed

So you've found a job. Congratulations! Here are a few tips to help you keep a job and protect you from future unemployment.

- Do an excellent job in the position you have.
- Set aside time each week to do things related to managing your career.
- Stay current in your chosen field by spending time reading and studying.
- Position yourself to accept more responsibilities.
- Get to know your boss. It is your responsibility to manage your relationship.
  - Build on your boss's strengths.
  - Find out your boss's and the organization's goals.
  - Find out early what is expected of you.
  - Discover your boss's tolerance of opposition and criticism.
  - Respect your boss's time.
  - Learn when your boss is most approachable.
  - Use tact, assertiveness, and common sense. Overcome inhibitions and take initiative. Remain nonthreatening.
  - Find out whether your boss takes risks.
  - Learn how receptive he or she is to new ideas.
- Evaluate yourself. Do you:
  - Solve problems before they reach your boss's desk?
  - Act independently?
  - Take initiative?
  - Handle crises and make tough decisions?
  - Have perspective and vision; understand the long-range goals of the organization? How have you helped to reach those goals?
  - Know that good mistakes come from exploring new territory?
  - Look to the needs of the organization?
  - Maintain regular contact with your boss?

Promotions

Remember, promotions are given not to reward past efforts but to solve tomorrow's problems. Be sure that your responsibility increases stay ahead of your salary increases.

Once you have successfully negotiated the job search process, do not let your skills go unused. Continue to research the job market in your field and make contacts with potential employers. You will always have opportunities to consider. If your supervisor discovers that you are exploring other possibilities and if you are doing a good job for your present company, he or she will know you are an excellent employee and that you have a chance to stay or leave.

Appendix II

Reviewing What You've Read

As you look over the questions below, decide whether you have covered the topic to your satisfaction. If not, go back to review the appropriate chapters in the guide.

Handling Your Job Loss

- Have you accepted the loss of your job and begun to take control of your life?
- Are you keeping yourself fit for the job search process ahead by taking such steps as avoiding isolation, joining a support group, and incorporating any necessary attitude adjustments?
- Are you following the recommended steps to handle stress and keep your self-esteem high?

Managing Your Personal Resources

- Are you making a schedule for your job search activities and sticking to it?
- Have you made a realistic financial plan to provide you and your family sufficient income while job hunting?
- Have you taken steps to ensure that you have health insurance?

Assessing Your Skills, Experience, and Interests

- Have you done a thorough self-assessment of your skills, knowledge, abilities, interests, values, and personality traits?
- Have you considered how personal and family considerations will affect your choice of a career?
- Are you able to think of some possible careers that you could do well and would like?

Researching the Job Market

- Have you identified the geographical areas and industries where your kind of work is likely to be found?
- Have you considered the possibility of relocating?
- Have you identified organizations that have your kind of work locally? nationally? overseas?

Conducting the Job Search

- Have you narrowed down the list of organizations to a manageable number in order to concentrate your job search efforts?
- Have you used all your resources, including the library and networking, to acquire information about the organizations you've targeted?
- Have you planned an effective campaign (mail, phone, or in person) to identify and develop job openings?

Networking

- Have you contacted everyone you know to tell them you're looking for a job? Have you overlooked anyone?
- Are you keeping track of all your networking contacts and following up on job leads obtained from them?
- Have you made an effort to expand your network by meeting or contacting new people?

Writing Resumes and Cover Letters

- Have you decided whether the functional or reverse chronological resume is best for you?
- Have you thoroughly inventoried your skills and accomplishments to determine which ones to emphasize in your resume?
- Have you proofread your resume carefully for spelling, grammar, and punctuation?

Employment Interviewing

- Have you prepared in advance so that you know what the employer wants and how your skills and abilities fit in with the organization's objectives?
- Have you practiced your interviewing techniques so that you can present yourself to your best advantage?
- Are you evaluating each interview afterward so that you can learn from the experience?
- Are you prepared to negotiate a salary?

Employment Testing

- Are you aware of the different types of tests employers may ask you to take?
- Do you know how to prepare for the different types of tests which you may encounter?

Sources of Additional Information

Following is a list of useful resource materials. Many can be purchased at a bookstore, and most can be found in a major library. More specialized materials (such as some government releases) may be obtained through the interlibrary loan office at your local library.

Materials are arranged by major topic. Listings that are highly recommended and of particular importance are set in bold type for the entire listing. Items with an asterisk are either published or distributed by JIST (the publisher of this book) and can be obtained directly from the publisher or through most bookstores.

Information on Careers and Industries

Occupational Outlook Handbook **(OOH).** Washington, DC: Dept. of Labor, Bureau of Labor Statistics. Revised every two years and available from most libraries, describes about 250 jobs covering 85% of the workforce.

America's Top 300 Jobs. Indianapolis: JIST Works, Inc. This is a bookstore version of the OOH that contains the same information and is revised every two years.

Guide for Occupational Exploration. (GOE). Washington, DC: Dept. of Labor. Originally published in 1979 and now superceded by the newer EGOE and CGOE that follow.

The Enhanced Guide for Occupational Exploration (EGOE). Indianapolis, JIST Works, Inc., 1991. Arranges about 2,500 jobs descriptions into 12 major interest areas and increasingly specific work groups. Useful for career exploration, identifying skills used in previous jobs, researching new job targets, and in preparing for interviews.

The Complete Guide for Occupational Exploration (CGOE). Indianapolis: JIST Works, Inc. 1993. Using the same organizational structure as the EGOE and GOE, lists more than 12,000 jobs.

Savage, K., & C. Dorgan, *Professional Careers Sourcebook, an Informational Guide for Career Planning.* Detroit: Gale Research, 1989.

Career Guide to America's Top Industries. Indianapolis: JIST Works, Inc., 1992. Information on over 40 major industries. Designed to help job seekers identify alternative job targets and to prepare for interviews.

U.S. Industrial Outlook. Washington, DC: Dept. of Commerce. Updated annually, lists all major industries and trends.

Dictionary of Occupational Titles (DOT). Washington DC: Dept. of Labor, 1991. Lists brief descriptions for more than 12,000 jobs. Useful for identifying skills used in past jobs, preparing for interviews, and identifying job targets.

All of the following cover specific aspects of the labor market and are by JIST Works, Inc., Indianapolis.

America's 50 Fastest Growing Jobs
America's Federal Jobs
America's Top Office, Management, and Sales Jobs
America's Top Medical and Human Service Jobs
America's Top Military Careers
America's Top Technical and Trade Jobs
America's Top Jobs for College Graduates

Emotional

Benson, Herbert, & Miriam Z. Klipper. *The Relaxation Response.* New York: Avon, 1976.

Branden, Nathaniel. *How to Raise Your Self-Esteem.* New York: Bantam Books, 1988.

Burns, David D. *Feeling Good Handbook.* New York: New American Libary-Dutton, 1990.

Charlesworth, Edward A., & Ronald G. Nathan. *Stress Management—A Comprehensive Guide to Wellness.* New York: Ballantine Books, 1984.

Ellis, Albert, & Robert A. Harper. *A New Guide to Rational Living.* North Hollywood, Calif: Wilshire Book Co., 1975.

Hanson, Peter, G. *Stress for Success: Dr. Peter Hanson's Prescription for Making Stress Work for You.* New York: Doubleday, 1989.

Sarnoff, Dorothy. *Never Be Nervous Again.* New York: Ivy Books, 1989.

Satir, Virginia. *Self-Esteem.* Berkeley, Calif: Celestial Arts, 1975.

Job Seeking & General

*Beatty, Richard H. *The Complete Job Search Book.* New York: John Wiley & Sons, 1988.

Bolles, Richard N. *How to Create Your Ideal Job or Next Career.* Berkeley, Calif: Ten Speed Press, 1989.

*Bolles, Richard N. *The Three Boxes of Life and How to Get Out of Them.* Berkeley, Calif: Ten Speed Press, 1991.

*Bolles, Richard N., *What Color Is Your Parachute? A Practical Manual for Job-Hunters & Career-Changers.* Berkeley, Calif: Ten Speed Press, revised annually. This is the best-selling career planning book of all time.

Danna, Jo. *Starting Over: You in the New Workplace.* Palomino Press, 1990.

Directory of Executive Recruiters, 1992. Fitzwilliam, NH: Kennedy, 1991.

*Farr, J. Michael. *The Very Quick Job Search: Get a Good Job in Less Time.* Indianapolis: JIST Works, Inc., 1991. This is the book we would recommend to a friend who is out of work. Proven techniques to plan careers and to reduce the time needed to find a job. Thorough.

*Figler, Howard E. *The Complete Job Search Handbook: All the Skills You Need to Get Any Job, and Have a Good Time Doing It.* New York: Henry Holt, 1988. A very good book.

Half, Robert. *How to Get a Better Job in This Crazy World.* New York: Crown, 1990.

*Jackson, Tom. *Guerilla Tactics in the New Job Market.* New York: Bantam Books, 1991.

The Job Bank Guide to Employment Services. Holbrook, Mass: Bob Adams, 1991.

*Lathrop, Richard. *Who's Hiring Who.* Berkeley, Calif: Ten Speed Press, 1989. Another good book.

LeCompte, Michelle. *Job Hunters Sourcebook: Where to Find Employment Leads and Other Job Search Sources.* Detroit: Gale Research, 1991.

Leeds, Dorothy. *Marketing Yourself: The Ultimate Job Seeker's Guide.* New York: Harper Collins, 1991.

Levering, Robert, Milton Moskowitz, & Michael Katz. *The 100 Best Companies to Work for in America.* New York: New American Library, 1992.

*Ludden, LaVerne, & Bonnie Maitlen. *Mind Your Own Business—Getting Started as an Entrepreneur.* Indianapolis: JIST Works, Inc., 1993

*Petras, Kathryn Ross. *The Only Job Hunting Guide You'll Ever Need.* New York: Poseiden Press, 1989.

*Stoodley, Martha. *Information Interviewing: What It Is and How to Use It in Your Career.* Garrett Park, Md: Garrett Park Press, 1990.

*Wegmann, Robert, & Robert Chapman. *The Right Place at the Right Time: Finding a Job in the 1990's.* Berkeley, Calif: Ten Speed Press, 1990.

*Wegmann, Robert, Robert Chapman, & Miriam Johnson. *Work in the New Economy: Careers and Job Seeking into the 21st Century.* Indianapolis: JIST Works Inc., 1989.

Job Search Manual. Baltimore, Md: White Ridgely Associates, 1992.

Interview

Beatty, Richard H. *The Five Minute Interview.* New York: John Wiley & Sons, 1986.

Caple, John. *The Ultimate Interview: How to Get It, Get Ready, and Get the Job You Want.* New York: Doubleday, 1991.

Hellman, Paul. *Ready, Aim, You're Hired!: How to Job-Interview Successfully Anytime, Anywhere, With Anyone.* New York: AMACOM, 1986.

Medley, H. Anthony. *Sweaty Palms Revised: The Neglected Art of Being Interviewed.* Berkeley, Calif: Ten Speed Press, 1991.

Yate, Martin John. *Knock 'em Dead: With Great Answers to Tough Interview Questions.* Holbrook, Mass: Bob Adams, 1992.

Yeager, Neil, & Lee Hough. *Power Interviewing: Job Winning Tactics From Fortune 500 Recruiters.* New York: John Wiley & Sons, 1990.

International

Kocher, Eric. *International Jobs: Where They Are, How to Get Them: A Handbook for Over 500 Career Opportunities Around the World.* Reading, Mass: Addison-Wesley, 1989.

*Krannich, Ronald L. & Caryl Rae Krannich. *The Complete Guide to International Jobs and Careers: Your Passport to a World of Exciting and Exotic Employment.* Manassass, Va: Impact Publications, 1990.

Resumes

Cohen, Hiyaguha. *The No Pain Resume Workbook.* Homewood, Ill: Business One Irwin, 1992.

*Jackson, Tom. *The Perfect Resume.* New York: Doubleday, 1990.

Karson, Allan. *Ready, Aim, Hired: Developing Your Brand Name Resume.* Homewood, Ill: Business One Irwin, 1991.

*Krannich, Ronald L., & Caryl Rae Krannich. *Dynamite Cover Letters.* Manassass, Va: Impact Publications, 1992.

*Krannich, Ronald L., & Caryl Rae Krannich. *Dynamite Resumes.* Manassass, Va: Impact Publications, 1992.

*Parker, Yana. *The Damn Good Resume Guide.* Berkeley, Calif: Ten Speed Press, 1989.

Swanson, David. *The Resume Solution.* Indianapolis: JIST Works, Inc., 1991.

Yate, Martin John. *Resumes That Knock'em Dead.* Holbrook, Mass: Bob Adams, 1988.

Salary Negotiation

Dawson, Roger. *You Can Get Anything You Want.* New York: Simon and Schuster, 1987.

Korda, Michael. *Success!* New York: Ballentine Books, 1978.

Tarrant, John. *Perks and Parachutes.* The Stone Song Press, 1985.

Testing

National Academy of Sciences. *Fairness in Employment Testing.* Washington, DC: National Academy Press.

Special Interest

Disabled Workers

Bolles, Richard N. *Job-Hunting Tips for the So-Called Handicapped or People Who Have Disabilities.* Berkeley, Calif: Ten Speed Press, 1991.

Klein, Karen, & Carla Derrick Hope. *Bouncing Back From Injury: How to Take Charge of Your Recuperation.* Rocklin, Calif: Prima Publishing, 1988.

Lewis, Adele, & Edith Marks. *Job Hunting for the Disabled.* Hauppauge, NY: Barron's Educational Series, 1983.

McCarthy, Henry [ed.]. *Complete Guide to Employing Persons with Disabilities.* Alberson, NY: Human Resource Center

National Rehabilitation Information Center, 8455 Colesville Road, Suite 935, Silver Spring, Maryland 20910-3319. (800) 346-2742; TDD 301-588-9284.

High-Tech Careers

Collard, Betsy A. *The High-Tech Career Book.* Los Altos, Calif: Crisp Publications, 1991.

Moore, David J. *Job Search for Technical Professionals.* New York: John Wiley & Sons, 1991.

The Hidden Job Market: A Job Seekers Guide to America's 2000.

Little Known, Fastest Growing High-Tech Companies. Princeton, NJ: Peterson's Guides, 1991.

MBAs

Holton, Ed. *The MBA's Guide to Career Planning.* Princeton, NJ: Peterson's Guides, 1989.

Minorities

*Johnson, Willis L. [ed.]. *Directory of Special Programs for Minority Group Members: Career Information Services, Employment Skills Banks, Financial Aid Services.* Garrett Park, Md: Garrett Park Press, 1990.

Nonprofit

McAdam, Terry W. *Doing Well by Doing Good: The First Complete Guide to Careers in the Non-Profit Sector.* Detroit: The Taft Group, 1986.

Smith, Devon C. *Great Careers: The Fourth of July Guide to Careers, Internships and Volunteer Opportunities in the Nonprofit Sector.* Garrett Park, Md: Garrett Park Press, 1990.

Older Workers

Bird, Caroline. *Second Careers: New Ways to Work After 50.* Boston: Little, Brown & Co., 1992.

*Birsner, E. Patricia. *The 40+ Job Hunting Guide (Official Handbook of the 40+ Club).* New York: Facts on File, 1990.

Morgan, John S. *Getting a Job After 50.* Petrocelli Books, 1990.

Ray, Samuel. *Job Hunting After 50: Strategies for Success.* New York: John Wiley & Sons, 1991.

Women

Chastain, Sherry. *Winning the Salary Game: Salary Negotiations for Women.* New York: John Wiley & Sons, 1980.

Koltnow, Emily, & Lynne S. Dumas, *Congratulations! You've Been Fired: Sound Advice for Women Who've Been Terminated, Pink Slipped, Downsized or Otherwise Unemployed.* New York: Fawcett Columbine, 1990.

Index